...ther there is no

GOODMAN

CONTENTS.

Published in 2009 by Goodman
An imprint of the
Carlton Publishing Group
20 Mortimer Street
London W1T 3JW

10 9 8 7 6 5 4 3 2 1

ISBN 978 1 84796 011 5

Printed and bound in China

Senior Executive Editor: Lisa Dyer
Creative Director: Clare Baggaley
Picture Researcher: Jenny Lord
Copy Editor: Lara Maiklem
Production: Kate Pimm

HALF TITLE PAGE Icon Brickell, Miami.
TITLE PAGE Interior by Kelly Hoppen.
PREVIOUS PAGE The lobby at Dwell 95
New York City.
RIGHT The Mondrian Hotel, Miami.

INTRODUCTION by
JOHN HITCHCOX

THE HOME IS SO IMPORTANT. It's about all of the things that stimulate happiness and contentment, family, love, care, children, leisure, play. Your home should be open, interesting, inspiring, warm, friendly and comfortable, a real place where you can live and work. These are the things that most of us want and this is what we are seeking to achieve at Yoo.

This book is about what we've learnt from having looked at people and their homes, in many different countries, in all different fields of activity, for more than 30 years now. Philippe Starck and I founded Yoo in 2000, and what Yoo do is offer up ideas. We aim to bring choice, freedom, flexibility and difference by offering a stable of the best: Philippe Starck, Jade Jagger, Marcel Wanders and Kelly Hoppen, all interpreted through our own Yoo Design Studio. We have worked with each of these celebrated designers to create a series of palettes to choose from, and now the Yoo studio has created its own independent styles. We are not saying, "you've got to buy it", and we're definitely not saying, "there is only one way". This is simply a method of assisting you in identifying your own individual style.

This book is a collection of our work, a tool to stimulate you into thinking about the kind of things you want to surround yourself with at home. The function of all the images in this book, many of which are not pictures of actual interiors, is to ask the question: "does this resonate with me?" Look at an image that you love in order to provide a springboard for desire – such as a leather Chesterfield chair, which helps define the Club palette for instance, or a vibrant cityscape, which is Techno, because maybe that image will enable you to determine, pin down and set the agenda for what you want to see in your own home.

THINKING ABOUT THE HOME

You are what you eat; you are also nourished by your environment. I'm still shocked that we go to school and learn things, like periodic tables that we might never use again, but we are taught very little about the home: how to lay out and plan the space we live in and how we live, love and interact with other people. Then we look at our greatest desire, which is health, contentment or happiness, and realize our home plays a really important part in that, and yet we learn so little about it. That doesn't make sense to me.

OPPOSITE TOP An Inuit family inside their igloo dwelling at Baker Lake, Nunavut, Canada.

OPPOSITE Dinner time in 1976, in a working-class home near Brescia in the Lombardy region of Italy.

We strive to share some of our experience of the home today. Our business is to try to improve the quality of people's lives through design, and to raise awareness of the importance of the home as a platform from which you take off to enjoy life, happiness, the universe. An architect frequently stops design work at the front door, and it's almost taboo, and slightly demeaning, to get involved in interiors. My father was an architect, my grandfather a builder and developer, my career has been a hybrid of the two, and Yoo has taken us fully inside the home. Yoo is both designer and developer. We want people to ENJOY the process of creating their own home.

It doesn't have to be a fast process, it's a kind of evolution, and this evolution is what makes the whole experience so much more enjoyable. Don't pressurize yourself into getting everything done. Do what you feel like doing. Get your bed in, get your table and chair in, and then take it at your own pace.

The nice thing about our business is that, at a very basic level, it's about food and shelter, simple but essential. Over the years architecture has evolved, and developed more rapidly in some ways than interiors, because it is about putting the roof on, putting the walls up first, making sure the drains work, and that it is dry inside. So humanity has gone from basic shelter to architecture, then more recently to interiors. Although I am fine on the macro-planning of space, I have always felt unqualified and unsure on interiors, so in founding Yoo I have surrounded myself with those who have made it their lives. I reasoned that if I found interiors difficult, other people must be in the same position.

An increasing number of us are now self-employed and we can influence that conflict between work and play time – the boundaries are increasingly blurred. Like many of us, I don't make the distinction between work and play: there's no fear of Fridays and I love Monday mornings. I don't need an office anymore – a lot of people don't need an office anymore, and the home and the workplace have melded into one. It's about finding a sense and ease of productivity without pressure, a sort of pull rather than a push.

In my life, work, leisure and play have pretty much no distinction, and therefore my home has always been very open plan. I enjoy stretching the eye, the long view. Designing the home around the individual is increasingly important, because it allows you to structure yourself in a more positive way – you might close off the dining area with a sliding door for a one-to-one meeting or to make an important call, then open it up again for lunch, when the kids run in from school, or friends come round in the evening. Your home needs to function around you, that's the point of good design.

I constantly question what it is that makes a home individual. I look at things that I've got in my own home, and everything means something different. Objects inject individuality into the home. I've discovered how important it is to identify things that are specific to you. For example, I have a Masai necklace on my piano at home. It's from Kenya, and for me has more emotional than physical beauty, because I bought it with my mother and daughter on the most magnificent trip to Africa. When I look at the object it takes me back to all that was happening, a kind of sensorial photo album. The struggle has been where to put it aesthetically in the house, because it doesn't necessarily "fit". There happens to be a resonance in the orange colour of the necklace: I have an orange candelabra, and orange dining chairs, so it works. That necklace is about colour, life, experience, travel and Africa, because I love Africa, but then again I wouldn't necessarily have an African-themed room.

"Philippe and I founded Yoo in 2000. I wanted to create a business that focused on the interiors of our homes, and Philippe was the obvious person to partner with. He's the most prolific and celebrated designer today. Right from the beginning we decided we wanted to give people a wealth and spectrum of styles to choose from, and stimulate them, without being prescriptive. Philippe came up with the name 'Yoo' – it's all about you, your life, your home; it's not about us. We were looking for a name that was short, descriptive and fun. So many other people would have simply put their name on the door, when in actual fact it should be your name on the door, not mine."

ABOVE John Hitchcox and Philippe Starck, founders of Yoo.

OPPOSITE The traditional nuclear-family home in 1959 – the doorway is a setting for arrivals and departures.

"The Downtown JP Morgan building had a lot of nostalgia and sentiment attached to it. It was JP Morgan's original office, and we started the conversion immediately after 9/11; there was a real need to revitalize the area at that time. The whole project was steeped in history, but there was also a sense of looking forward, of creating a new community within the walls of this otherwise empty urban space."

TOP A 1,900-piece Louis XV chandelier that originally hung in the banking hall of the JP Morgan building has been reassembled in the lobby at Downtown by Starck, where it hovers inches above the floor.

ABOVE A Jon Male table in the gold "vault" room in the Downtown by Starck building in the financial district.

It's about collectibles, and the emotional value that you attach to each object. Our approach is about giving people the confidence and sense of security to achieve this rare individuality. The idea of how you present yourself to the world is very strongly linked to your home. Our role is to try to create the most soothing, loving, caring, humorous and harmonious environment we can, in order to achieve happiness. We are not in any way trying to restrict, predetermine or institutionalize how people lay out their furniture. We are simply saying: "This is our experience, but do what you want. It's your home."

BUILDING THE HOME

The basic house model was designed hundreds of years ago. In the 1930s, '40s and '50s house design changed and moved forward, and the 1960s saw a mushrooming of modern housing. There's been a lot of urban development since then, and cities have rapidly expanded, especially in the last ten years or so.

I've been involved in building homes for people for the last thirty years, and in that time a huge amount of urbanization has taken place. People are moving back into the cities. Over the past ten years, my life has been a bit like an astronaut: I've been landing in new cities and looking at them, analyzing the way they evolve, their structure, regeneration and growth.

One of Yoo's roles has been to recreate the village in an urban setting. Sometimes we describe our buildings as "vertical villages" where you have everything you normally have in your local village. The pub, the library, the coffee shop, whatever it might be, all of that is on the ground floor, and above that you have all the homes. This has worked especially well in America – I've seen a situation in the Yoo Icon South Beach building in Miami, for instance, where the recording artist met the accountant, who met the graphic designer (who all now work together in some form) in the downstairs residents' bar watching football one evening. What's lovely about this is that so often in these urban settings you don't even know your neighbour, let alone meet up with them or work alongside them. In building these urban communities, Yoo strives to create a sanctuary within a densely populated environment.

In the majority of our projects we incorporate interactive communal spaces in a very proactive way: a clubroom, a library or study, pool table or swimming pool. In the Downtown New York building we have a vertical playground. We have Playstations, we have basketball, we have squash courts and climbing frames; something different on each level. There is a big difference between hotels and homes – you're only in a hotel for a couple of days but a home is for life. The commonality is the lobby, but you must recognize the difference between the short stay for the customers versus the elegance and permanence of a living room. The concept of moving through a communal space has more value today than it ever had. A beautiful lobby in a building allows the transition between the outside world and your inner space.

OPPOSITE An exterior view of Downtown by Starck on Broad Street, New York City. An example of "vertical" living, the building comprises a landscaped roof terrace with intimate seating areas and a large pool fed by a giant water tap, as well as a fitness centre and an indoor lounge. The view from the terrace looks directly at the historical pediment of the New York Stock Exchange.

All Yoo projects are different throughout the world (we know, for example, you can't build a bathroom in Argentina without a bidet in it), but there is a general theme around circulation, the use of space and an open-plan environment. If you take an eighteenth-century French apartment, you can never see the kitchen because it's always right at the other end of the floor plan, whereas now the kitchen has become a much more central feature, and that's almost universal – it applies across the world today.

My entire life is about building things that I would like to live in. It's the only thing I identify with: you are what you know. I tend to build what I would like, and assume, or hope, that if I like it then others might too.

I am always a bit wary of the word "brand", it's a new word for me but what it describes is a group of people with similar thoughts and a producer who services or provides for that group of customers, that is to say his "community". Globalization means that within each Yoo building we have a collective, a group of people who are all similar thinkers, like-minded: that is our customer. So a lot of people are moving into our buildings, and immediately, and quite naturally, they create a community.

"What I really love about Hong Kong is the elegant hustle and bustle, the fantastic street life. Causeway Bay is this little jewel in a city that is really like New York, without the aggression. There's a wonderful level of activity, but also a calmness and peace surrounding the place. We took what was an old serviced apartment building and brought it back to life in a new and very ethereal way."

OPPOSITE Causeway Bay, Hong Kong, teams with activity and street life.

BELOW A serene retreat from the vibrant Causeway Bay: an apartment at the Jia, Hong Kong, is sheltered from the outside world with floor-to-ceiling sheer curtains.

"There is a club element that exists within the brand itself;
The Lakes by Yoo is a brilliant example of this, people are moving
there not only for the obvious reasons of the beautiful design,
countryside and scenery, but because they have like-minded
neighbours. They are second homes, weekend places, but these are
still a bunch of people who all think in a similar way. It's not
about just packing the kids in the car on a Friday night, and then
finding all they do is sit in their rooms and play Nintendo or go
on Facebook. It's a place where kids go fishing, sailing, camping
together with mates they've met there. It's a great environment
for urbanites to experience and enjoy the countryside."

GLOBALIZATION

Increasingly, Yoo's role is to distribute designers as widely as we can, and get involved in a big geographical spread of development. We're currently working on projects in over thirty countries. We have apartments, offices and hotel spaces all over Central and South America, we're working in Russia and everywhere in between, so there appears to be a global appetite for what we're doing. At the same time, we want to remain completely accessible and democratic.

> We want to demystify the whole idea of interior design. Value is the new form of desire, and design is more value-conscious now than it ever has been.

In terms of design and the way people live in the places we've been working in, the furniture, layouts and much of what people aspire to has become very similar, very quickly, across the entire globe. Still when I go to China I sit on a massive chair, and when I go to India I sit on something quite different, so there remains quite obvious cultural differences, though I think these are diminishing. The same products are sent across the world. People are as familiar with a Starck chair in America as they are in Singapore or Hong Kong.

There's a certain type of person that's been around the globe and has seen the way other people live, and want to be part of that. What we're doing is presenting that locally. There are definitely cultural idiosyncrasies, but beyond that there is a global sense of design. We like to start off with the local culture, then introduce our work. We go round and have a look at everything we can. We've collected ideas from all over the world, and that shows in the body of our work.

So, this is what we've been doing over the last ten years. We've reached a point where we can show how we've thought out things, and share our experience. Yoo is not elitist, and hopefully there's a certain DIY value in this book. It's all part of the democratization of design. Everybody's ideas are valuable. I hope this book helps to crystallize yours.

TOP A group of brightly clothed Masai women standing outside a hut in a village on the Masai Mara National Reserve, Rift Valley, Kenya.

CENTRE Uros children play near their reed home at Uros island on Lake Titicaca at the border of Bolivia and Peru.

LEFT Jade Jagger researching locally crafted prints and textiles in India.

OPPOSITE TOP AND BOTTOM Tipis outside the Lakes by Yoo in the Cotswolds, England. The contemporary glass and wood homes are integrated into the surrounding landscape, and embody a synthesis between nature and the individual.

"With Jade, we recognized her distinct style as a personality, and also her style in designing her own homes. Everyone else we work with is a dedicated interior designer, but Jade was able to come at it from a completely fresh and different angle. She had the particular experience of designing jewellery and so when we brought her to our design studio she came up with the idea of an oversized jewelbox for her first apartments in New York – a lacquered pod in the middle of the space, with a bathroom, kitchen and closet in it. It was about taking the essence of Jade's spirit and personality, and creating something we'd never done before."

TOP Jade Jagger. BELOW Marcel Wanders.
OPPOSITE Philippe Starck with John Hitchcox
in the background.

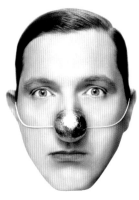

OVERLEAF The library at G-Tower in Dubai,
a public area for all residents.

DESIGNERS AND THE CULT OF CELEBRITY

We seem to attach ourselves to characters today. People identify with the interior behind the person. Yoo are the producer, we are the implementer of these personality-driven designs around the world. The relationship Yoo and I have with each of our designers has always started on a very personal level. I met Philippe in Paris because he knew my next-door neighbour. I first met Jade on holiday in Mustique, and I was introduced to Marcel at a restaurant in Holland. I've known Kelly for years, and realized that getting her involved with Yoo was an opportunity to broaden our spectrum with a comfortable but clean, classic style. Today we offer 18 different style palettes, but this book isn't here to persuade you to choose a single style that you identify with most. Our aim is to guide you into creating something that's completely unique, rare and individual to you.

The whole concept of superstar designers is really a way of identifying what people might like in their interiors. What we aren't doing is assuming a Big Brother cult of celebrity, attaching a cursory label or brand to individuals with nothing else to offer. My notion of celebrity is somewhat old-fashioned – I guess it's a generational thing. For me it's about people who are famous for what they have done, what they have produced and what they have achieved, who have a profile and an identity which can ultimately be defined in an interior. We are simply recognizing this, and acknowledging it. It's the idea that we are defined by the things we love, by the people we admire and the objects we surround ourselves with in our own home, and it has always been there, though not necessarily exposed in such an obvious way.

We are definitely trying to bring a sense of diversity into our stable of designers, and Philippe is distinctly different from Marcel, Jade is very much more hippy, whereas Kelly is more Zen. One of the common themes with all these designers, however, is their recognition of modern-day marketing, that media presentation is all important. Starck creates ways to present his product to the public, which are very media-friendly, like the image of him hanging himself up on his own hook design. Starck's entire visual presentation is one which is humorous, intellectual, immediate and visual. Marcel recognizes that, so do Jade and Kelly. They all give time, effort and thought to the process of marketing and selling their products.

> Good design is about entertainment, not just functionality, and these celebrity designers inherently understand that. Aesthetics is visual entertainment. Humanity, fun and humour are the core values.

These designers cover and have designed some of the most popular pieces of furniture in the world. Our reason for using them is not because they are famous names – the fact that they are names at all is an aside. It's fair to say that in the spectrum of housing, our attention to design is second to none, but it's also true that the idea we have of this line-up of superstars definitely gets us more attention. The information age of today, with the Internet and Facebook, has allowed people to create celebrities, and some of them do things, some of them don't. What you are getting is this band of like-minded people, this globalization of tribes, because they recognize and appreciate certain people's skill sets, fortes, tastes, whatever it might be. Celebrity and brand are interestingly synonymous. The diversity of individuality is that much greater, you grab ideas from all over the place, and all of that is to do with the information age.

CULTURE.

pompidou
andy warhol
mini cooper
movie
artifice
jewellery
media
explosion
neon lights
baroque colour
the stuff that surrounds you
gilded and grounded
flea market
eccentric

yoo inspired by STARCK

CULTURE

Philippe Starck has developed a number of palettes for Yoo, as he explains: "The family of Yoo styles has been put together so that we can help people to make the right choices. The process works by showing people a selection of different images that relate to the home, different furniture or materials or other objects. They start to make their choices, selecting certain things they like and don't like. From this it is easy to see what sort of person they are and what they will like." For Starck, the palettes don't have to be used as a single style in one apartment, he likes to mix and match. "I love the style we call Culture, but this is not to the exclusion of the others. I like my dressing room very Classic, my kitchen in the style of Nature, my salon as Culture and my bedroom very sexy."

For Starck, the Culture palette is genuinely eclectic – "it is a mix of everything good. I urge anyone using this to be confident, make a selection of all the things you love and bring them together." The palette evolved by exploring what we mean by the word culture. For Starck this unites art, music, literature, history, travel and more. By understanding the component parts it is possible to combine them to create rooms with many layers of decoration. "Don't be afraid of the bizarre, this is a flea market or a souk, a mix of everything that's beautiful."

The Culture palette epitomizes much of Starck's. It encapsulates his passion for appropriating the most beautiful and exquisitely produced objects and ideas from the past, and placing them alongside the most amazing designs of today. The result is an intriguing mix that has a captivating tension. We can see this in so many of his public interiors where antique furniture and furnishings, especially anything from the reign of Louis XV, sit alongside Venetian glass mirrors, ornately carved stone fireplaces, shimmering chandeliers and pre-nineteenth century paintings, all enlivened by the arrival of glittering gold stools surreally cast in the shape of a head, a plastic table lamp, a tribal warrior's mask and perhaps a curious chair made from animal horns and a dappled pelt. This highly energizing mix is now finding a life in his Culture palette for homes, which by no means diminishes the effect in any way.

Starck suggests that the person most interested in this palette could be a collector and is certainly someone who enjoys indulgence. "He or she is confident and daring, maybe a little crazy, and not afraid to mix colours and styles. Instinctively, they will know it is OK to have an Arne Jacobsen chair next to something in the style of Louis XV, and then to add a Picasso." The Culture palette is rooted in richness and boldness and has a powerful sense of history, but it is also always looking forward.

Homage to the Old Masters

Key to this style is its drama. Colours are used with daring accents and contrasts, lighting mixes subtle washes with bold hotspots of brightness, and there is a playful use of scale, particularly in the use of huge images or mirrors and vases that are so tall

ABOVE The deep, rich Culture palette includes limestone, steamed beech and sisal, along with deep purples and oriental reds.

OPPOSITE A communal living room at the Icon South Beach showcases an African-designed chair in an otherwise traditionally American-style living decor. In the bookshelves are Philippe Starck's Miss Sissi moulded plastic lamps, manufactured by Flos in a wide range of colours.

they almost reach the ceiling and oversize the other furniture. What makes this palette most remarkable is its homage to the paintings of the Old Masters, with their beautiful and often highly seductive subjects and use of pigment-rich colours. Starck's interiors themselves are also fine compositions. Rooted in his love of symmetry and order, they have a powerful central focus (a fireplace, mirror or painting), complementary colours that are used as a backdrop, and an accent of contrasting colour. There are also intriguing textures, and bold gestures in the shape of velvet curtains or an oversize mirror. And then there are delightful details: exquisite wine glasses and elegant cutlery. Every room is a picture with its layers of texture.

Old Masters is a term that usually refers to European artists, such as Caravaggio, Vermeer and Ingres, who worked in the sixteenth, seventeenth and eighteenth centuries. Starck especially admires Ingres' famous nude, the *Grand Odalisque*, with her warm skin tones that are offset by cobalt-turquoise coloured silk and rich ochre velvet. These intense pigment colours feature regularly in the Culture rooms, where deep colours are often used as a backdrop against which citrus spikes of lime green, lemon yellow or orange are added to heighten the experience. "This is very theatrical and intellectual and fun," says Starck. "It is possible to have purple and orange close together because you know it is a very good purple and a very good orange."

Within this world of intense and gorgeous colour, the furniture and furnishings include glinting mirrors with a decorative flourish crowning the frame; fine furniture with flamboyant, carved scrollwork picked out in gold and silver; delicate needlepoint Aubusson rugs with their faded rose patterns; and always books. The Culture fan will certainly want to be surrounded by books, and even where the real thing might be in short supply Starck will choose a charming and effective book wallpaper to evoke an atmosphere of learning and studiousness.

Finally, the drama is heightened with expert lighting. "Without light we do not exist. Light is all," says Starck. "Without light everything is black and nothing. In the Middle Ages, when light was rare and precious, we did everything we could to capture it and reflect it in metals and jewels and glass. The king was the most important person in the world because he was surrounded by light and reflected light. Poor people could not be seen and so did not exist. It is only in the modern day, when we have so much artificial light that we start to wear black. I like the mystery of shadow and translucency." One of Starck's most daring and amazing recent interiors is finished almost entirely in a rich and enticing gold, complete with gold wall tiles, gilt furniture and glimmering chandeliers. With his astonishingly expert use of lighting, Starck succeeds in turning the space into an enchanting fairy-tale interior, warm and womb-like, yet also glamorous.

OPPOSITE TOP A private meeting room at the Gramercy, New York. A Muletas lamp by Salvador Dalí, originally designed in 1937, in carved varnished limewood appears on the left.

OPPOSITE A cinema screening room in the Icon Vallarta, Puerto Vallarta, Mexico, with a chandelier of reindeer antlers.

RIGHT TOP TO BOTTOM Communal residence areas in the Icon Brickell in Miami. Custom-made furniture provide seating while enlarged classic images, in the style of Old Masters, adorn the walls, creating dramatic focus in the rooms and adding a spirit of fun. An overscaled white vase by Pols Potten heightens the visual excitement in the bottom image.

ABOVE The entrance to the lobby at the Icon Brickell. Stage-lit mood lighting creates a vignette in the shadows with a floral needlepoint rug by Rêves du Désert.

OPPOSITE Purpose-built bench seating with white leather and polished chrome is highlighted with neon lighting. Gold Bonze stools by Philippe Starck for XO stand guard. A sculpture, table or a stool, the Bonze has a totemic-like quality.

OVERLEAF Handpainted faux bookshelf wallpaper by Deborah Bowness lines the wall while silver aluminium blinds cover the windows in this monochromatic interior. An Asiatides black ceramic stool resides in the foreground next to a Maarten Baas Smoke armchair by Mooi and a white and gold porter's chair by Boffi. The modern classic La Chaise by Eames in white moulded plastic appears far right.

A Copenhagen bathroom is lined in Romany blue limestone tiles and lit with Romeo Babe lights by Philippe Starck for Flos.

A museum print is placed above the Sleepy Working Bed by Phillippe Starck for Cassina. A desk attaches to the headboard and dual bedside tables have power points with an additional table at the foot of the bed. Lights serve both bedside and desk positions.

ABOVE Vintage prints – here of tango partners – can be acquired from stock picture agencies and old magazines to provide inexpensive wall decoration. Centre stage is a Piero Fornasetti chair, lacquered and screenprinted with a pillar capital.

OPPOSITE The "vault" room at the former JP Morgan building, now Downtown by Starck. Gold mosaic tiles from Belgium cover the floors, walls and ceiling and a series of gold Bonze stools stand sentry. A Boffi portman's loveseat in gold is placed at the back of the room.

PHILIPPE STARCK

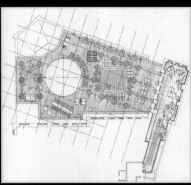

Along with being the world's most famous designer, you are also a philosopher, artist, comedian, psychiatrist, magician – do these different aspects help your creativity and keep your work fresh?

Creativity is a sickness. You cannot choose creativity, it chooses you. When you accept the deal, it's like Faust, you are selling your soul to the devil. You have no more life. Most people think they live to be happy, but in the field of creativity, you understand very fast that you are not in the world to be happy… you are in the world to just do it. I must be creative, it is like a duty, I have no choice. I am always involved with a project and so I have no concept of ordinary life or happiness. I am made of flesh and sweat, but life and happiness is for other people.

Can you remember when you first became interested in design?

I am not interested in design or architecture. I still don't really know why I do this job. When I was a young boy living with my mother we had very little furniture; I slept on the floor with no bed. Life went on like this until I was grown up. I didn't know a bed existed. I lived like a hippy sleeping on a piece of foam. Then one day I had the opportunity to share a bed with a very charming person and it was fantastic, so I discovered the bed. The same was true with the chair and every other piece of furniture. I discovered them one by one and decided to make my own bed and chair and table. I am a very hard worker and a good fighter, but part of me is also lazy. Designing is very easy for me, so it makes sense… why not do it?

So can you describe your interest in design?

I am not interested in design, but I am interested in designing. The real reason why I love designing is that I am passionate about our story; the story of the human species. This is a long story that started four billion years ago and will end in the coming four billion years. For me this story is like a movie or a book, and it has eight billion pages. I love this story, it is the most romantic and the most poetic I've ever read. I have a real sympathy for the bacteria we were four billion years ago and for the fish, the frog in the process, then the monkey and the super monkey we are today. I am so excited and so curious about the future. I want to try to understand what we shall become. How will we mutate before the sun implodes and we explode?

What is it about this story that captivates you so much?

It is a fantastic story of intelligence. I am the president of the fan club for human intelligence. I want to understand how and why one stupid animal decided to become intelligent and then went on to invent this civilization. I am fascinated by the idea of progress – we have to look very carefully at the dangerous concept of god, and the beautiful concept of love. This is my territory. I have X-ray eyes which can scan the beautiful story of human life and I can see this beautiful story in everything.

Can you describe how your curiosity about the human story relates to your design work?

It is directly related. Everything I do must fit within the bigger picture of this human story. Everything outside that frame is absolutely useless. No object or project deserves to exist if it doesn't serve the human mutation. Of course I don't always succeed. I can make mistakes and occasionally I can be stupid, but all my life I must use my tools as a designer to serve my fellow humans. That is my goal. I must use rigour and poetry and humour and ethics and honesty and vision. And I must work hard. This is the minimum I owe to civilization.

This sounds like a very tough deal. What drives you?

If we take the trouble to look and understand we will know that every one of us is part of a tribe. When you are born, you sign a contract with your tribe. If you are creative you must always work to help the species to evolve. I am sad not to be more useful. I'm sad that I'm not an important mathematician, a scientist, or an astrophysicist… but inside the bubble of my useless job, I have to do good things.

Can you describe how you do good things with space?

We can talk about public space and private space. Public space is about emotion and experience. As a designer of restaurants, bars and hotels, my job is like a film director, I have to tell a story and print the strongest memory of the spirit of the place on everyone who visits. I must use every tool available to astonish people and wake them up and provoke them and give them some energy.

For private spaces it is the opposite. I must be very humble and almost silent. I have to be a good friend who listens and helps people to build their own home and life. Then I must disappear. I provide them with a space that has the best-quality plan, the best proportions, the best volumes and the best materials. In private space my role is to protect the energy and love of the young couple or the family. Their job is to get on with their life.

You have a number of homes around the world, can you describe some of the qualities of your own homes?

I have to forget about myself and think only about other people night and day. I make projects for my tribe, I don't have time to think about me. Because I spend so much of my life on a plane, I think I am a spirit or a ghost. I live between the earth and the sky. Up there you have a different idea of what is a home. When I am not in the air, I stay in very minimal spaces, humble homes, cabanas. I am speaking to you now from my cabana in south-west France. It's on a small island and is just a wooden cabana with no electricity or running water or a car. I, with my wife, also stay sometimes in Venice in a humble fisherman's house, or a cabin in the forest. Each place is very simple. We have whatever furniture we can find, but most importantly of all, each place has a magical quality. They are in the middle of nowhere, very simple with large windows, so we are in the middle of nature.

When it comes to homes for most of us, can you describe how you think people's tastes have changed in recent years?

The best news is that there is no longer one way to think or to see. There has been an atomic explosion of different tastes and trends and people are now free to choose and live as they want to. It is the end of that big dictatorship of pursuing just one style.

How does this have an effect on your design work?

When it comes to furniture, I have won my personal battle for democratic furniture design. My mission was to find a way of raising quality and lowering prices and making well-designed chairs available for the maximum number of people. My first successful chair was the Café Costes, which sold for around $700. Every two years thereafter, I won the battle to halve the price of the chairs. There was Mr Blob which sold at around $300, followed by Lord Yo at $140 and Dr No at $100. Then there was La Marie which launched for less. Homes are a more complex challenge, so now I am in the process of making democratic architecture and I am creating prototypes for new-build homes. At the same time we have Yoo, which is a concept for living in apartments and making it easy for people to avoid costly mistakes and create their own home and life

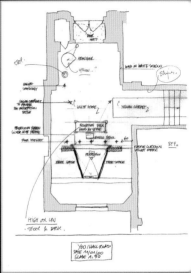

TOP The reception desk at the entrance lobby to the Yoo NW8 Building, in Hall Road, St John's Wood London. A converted 1930s telephone exchange, the apartments are available in four Starck palette – Culture, Classic, Nature and Minimal.

ABOVE Philippe Starck's sketch for the NW8 Building lobby, featuring the reception desk in the centre, opposite the door entrance at the top.

ECLECTIC.

colourful
contrast
surreal
style-mix
eccentric
decorative
pattern
gold

WANDERS & **yoo**

ECLECTIC

If there is one Yoo palette that best sums up Marcel Wanders' approach to design, it is Eclectic. Wanders' furniture and industrial designs are widely diverse in style and material, while his interiors are marked by a tendency to juxtapose different styles, patterns and forms together. "The Eclectic is very vibrant," Wanders exclaims. "It is the most eccentric, perhaps, out of the lot of them. It is one of the most colourful themes." Eclectic represents a palette where styles can be mixed and matched, and where elements from all the other themes can be shaken up together.

A look that's full of contrasts

Most of the interior projects Wanders has worked on to date could be described as eclectic, since different rooms and areas within them have often contained a variety of thematic approaches, which, when taken together, make up a look that is full of contrasts. "I think contrast would be a very important word," says Wanders. "There is a lot of contrast in what we do." Generally used to enliven a space, contrast in design terms is achieved by putting two or more elements in opposition to one another, such as black and white pillows on a sofa, or in opposition, such as circle and square forms or florals and geometrics, used together.

The Mondrian South Beach hotel and apartment complex, which opened on West Avenue in 2008 in Miami Beach and which is Wanders' largest interior project to date, is a perfect example of his use of contrasts. Overlooking Biscayne Bay and conceived as a "Sleeping Beauty's castle", this project features highly theatrical public spaces with over-scaled columns, decorative screens and surfaces patterned with contrasting mosaics, tiles and rugs. "There are parts of Mondrian South Beach that are very Architectural (see pages 58–63), the restaurant, for example, and there are spaces that are more like New Antiques (see pages 74–9), such as the entrance, and there are others that are more Eclectic." The way these different spaces are sequenced to constantly surprise and delight visitors indicates the way the four different themes are combined at Yoo developments.

Another example of an eclectic interior by Wanders is his work at the Kameha Grand Bonn hotel in Bonn, Germany, which opened in the autumn of 2009. The interiors of this luxury business hotel deliberately eschew the serious practical, and consequently boring, approach taken by most hotels of this type and instead aim to be, in Wanders' words, "a place full of surprises, of beauty and energy, a place that is sexy and cool". To break up the hotel's cavernous public areas, Wanders has utilized light, flowing materials that are suspended from the ceiling to create private "meeting islands". His trademark exaggerations of scale are also used to define the space and astonish users – these include giant columns printed with bands of pattern, over-scale chandeliers, and huge seating islands that are employed in the lounge area.

ABOVE Neutral colours ground vibrant colours and textures in the Eclectic palette. Flooring in Verona walnut or parquet is combined with decorative Couture wallpapers in red, black and yellow, Dynasty gold silk fabric, Bisazza mosaic tiles, stainless steel and high gloss paints.

OPPOSITE Eclectic themes work perfectly with fantasy elements. The Sleeping Beauty fairytale takes form in a laser-cut steel staircase which is the centrepiece in the lobby of the Mondrian South Beach. Wanders has famously likened the design approach to the hotel as "the moment when the story ends, and people wake up after a hundred years and see with new eyes".

RIGHT Highly decorated and textured surfaces are used to create a dramatic interior that is not for the faint-hearted. White objects, called topiaries, are in the style of Wanders' seminal Crochet table. The plaster ceiling shows a pattern that is reflected in the custom-made, wooden parquet flooring.

BELOW An effective use of contrast can be seen in the extroverted Eclectic palette. In this spa/bathing area oversized floral and stripe patterns are laid out in tiny black and white mosaic tiles, while crystal chandeliers light the showers. Taking items away from their traditional contexts gives a fresh perspective and adds the element of surprise.

However, the Eclectic palette is not a total free-for-all and, away from the showpiece public areas, the aim is to create comfortable homes that people want to live in. "We will be sure the theme works in a very homey way," Wanders says. "We want to make homes for people, we don't want to make carnival places." The keywords for the Eclectic theme are colourful, contrast, surreal, style-mix, eccentric, decorative, pattern and gold – the latter being a colour that will be used liberally. "We will use gold, why not?" says Wanders. "It's a beautiful colour!" And, as you would expect, the material palette for the Eclectic interiors is the most diverse of all Wanders' palettes. The floors in living areas are made of herringbone parquet and walnut, while in the bedrooms they are carpeted in tartan or floral patterns. In keeping with the Eclectic style, fabric is also used on feature walls, where they are finished in gold silk.

Lighting is also important and is designed in response to the interior layouts, and to draw attention to particular features and details. "I think you need lights on ideas and on details," says Wanders. "In certain areas we will give real direction to the light."

The Eclectic theme also responds well to the particular local styles of the city or country in which the Yoo development is located. Regional furnishings, patterns and materials can creep into the interiors to give them a particular local flavour. "We will try to mix local aspects and world aspects in this Eclectic palette," says Wanders. "If we are in China it makes sense to use Chinese inspiration. We could do something typically Chinese, or something inspired by something Chinese, but from a completely different point of view. This may give you some ideas on the contrast that we foresee."

We will be sure the theme works in a very homey way. We want to make homes for people, we don't want to make carnival places.

OVERLEAF The approach to the lobby design at the Kameha Grand Bonn hotel can be adapted to any large meeting area or living room that needs to serve multiple purposes. Here, the room was sectioned into intimate seating areas to encourage conversation and interaction and to move around or remove any time the large space needs to be reconfigured. High ceilings and glass walls allow the use of over-scaled pieces without compromising the feeling of spaciousness.

TOP An emphatic use of wallpaper on a single wall serves to create a focal point and add dynamic presence. The design is from Marcel's Couture collection for Graham & Brown, which features a strong mix of bold colourways and more subtle shades from vivid oranges and reds to rich golds and chocolates. Here, the Isabella combines large-scale Celtic motifs against a backdrop of tartan; the range includes a large diversity of original patterns.

ABOVE In this black and white bathroom, accented with red mosaic tiles in the toilet, a black lacquered Paris mirror by Wanders for Quodes is set against a wall that is covered with hand-carved wooden tiles, with a white Soapstars basin below. Part of his Beautiful Women range, which returns to a historical style, the mirror was designed for the bedroom, but can be used anywhere in the home. The layering of ornate detailing in the setting creates a visually exciting and opulent effect.

MINIMAL.

white
empty space
simple
pure
concrete
function
water
air
glass
smooth
clean
hard
shell
form

yoo inspired by STARCK

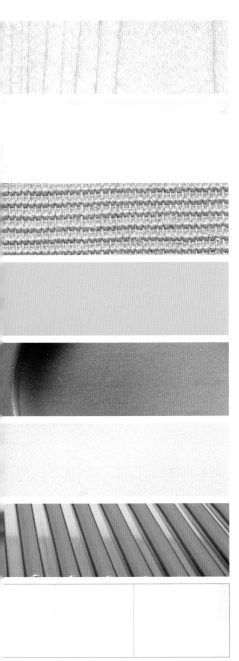

MINIMAL

Because Philippe Starck is rarely associated with the concept of minimal design, this palette is all the more intriguing. "I call it Minimal, not minimalist," stresses Starck. "Minimalist is a trend that is dead and gone. In a Minimal apartment every line and every material counts. We could be thinking about Japan and life in black and white. This is the essence of life."

This palette has grown from the urge that we all sometimes have for simplicity and a lack of complication. The Minimal palette is a breath of fresh air and looks good at a large and impressive scale, while also working particularly well in smaller rooms and apartments. The palette has a modern edge, incorporating glass, metal, concrete and neutral colours. However, there is always plenty of interest in textures and exciting combinations of objects and materials.

The spirit of this style is clean and calm. It is contemplative too. This sort of simplicity has a particular appeal for busy urbanites, people who have demanding jobs and a social calendar that is booked up weeks in advance. After a full day of challenging work, and then enjoying time with friends, what better way to finish the evening than to be cradled in a haven of calm? Here, surrounded by order and rational design that is softened with beautiful fabrics and subtle lighting, there is time and space to recharge. It might mean being enveloped and embraced by a beautiful Arne Jacobsen Egg chair as you become lost in a good book, enjoying the luxury of a beautifully finished, all-white bathroom, or drifting away in a bed made with fresh, crisp linen. The Minimal palette allows the mind to find space to meditate and consider.

The palette is ideal for those who want to add their own layers and ideas. It can work as a simple start in deciding how you want to live, an almost blank canvas where you can gradually add objects to reflect your own tastes and personality. One of its key strengths is that it looks great in its most basic form, and also acts as a fantastic backdrop to beautiful items and social events. Imagine sitting in a white room at a white dining table that is surrounded by white chairs… all the emphasis is on your guests and the food and wine.

A luxurious approach to minimalism

While Starck is often considered a maximalist, there's a minimal fan inside trying to break out. At his most reflective, he wants to get away from a life of plenty. "I think many, many people are ready to cast off their excess baggage," he says, counting himself among their number. But he also recognizes that a minimal life is associated with luxury. "Of course the hungry have no need to diet, but it will change. Eventually everyone will come to see that less really is more. We can all benefit if we consume less. Of course the idea will take longer to flower in some places than others. I used to be a pessimist, but now I am an optimist and believe

ABOVE The neutral Minimal palette uses Thassos quartz, white maple, sisal, wool textures, and pale yellow, as well as aluminium and stainless steel.

OPPOSITE TOP AND BOTTOM The gentle curved shape of Arne Jacobsen Egg chairs are ideally suited for a Minimal palette.

things will improve. I can be actively working on solutions instead of wasting energy feeling bad about the problems. I have faith in people."

Smooth and reflective surfaces are an important feature in this palette. They add a welcome lustre and air of luxury. Glass, of course, plays a major role and not just in the form of huge floor to ceiling windows that flood rooms with light, but also in details such as the trademark crystal chandeliers. Lighting is also extremely important, especially indirect lighting from table lamps and floor lamps that provide highlights, drawing the eye around the room.

All of these features have appeared in Starck's work over the years. There was the Minimum dining table, an elegant structure on splayed steel legs with a plate glass top; the monolithic white marble staircase for the Asahi Beer Hall in Tokyo, and the dozens of lamp designs that are always playing with new ways of washing walls or spotlighting objects. His brand of Minimal design is possibly best epitomized by his chair design called La Marie – an apparently simple design that is constructed in translucent plastic, but is impossible to ignore.

While minimalism is often associated with spartan, even chilly, interiors, Starck's Minimal palette is big on comfort and luxury. For example, it might include a room with white painted walls that has soft, white carpet underfoot, pale linen curtains that pick up the breeze, and sculptural furniture upholstered in the softest cream-coloured wool or leather. The overall effect is of a calm and controlled space, but it is not about denial.

As ever, in this palette there is also a splash of Starck's welcome subversion – look out for the hot spots of colour and the quirky use of imagery. These might include a sizzling, lipstick-red chair in an otherwise all-white room, unexpected pieces of sculpture, such as blackbirds perched on shelves that are set against a yellow backdrop; a huge portrait of a nude that is so large it climbs up the wall and then turns at 90 degrees to rest on the ceiling.

Always playing with our perceptions, one of Starck's great triumphs in the use of the Minimal style is the way he uses the limited palette to focus attention on one area or just a few objects. The life-size blackbird sculptures are one example, but another favourite is the all-white room – complete with white table, white chairs, white floor, white ceiling and glass chandelier – which features all-white bookshelves that hold a collection of bright-coloured paperback books. Set in their dreamlike white world, the books appear almost to be suspended in space. Although the style might be called Minimal, it can have maximum impact.

Eventually everyone will come to see that less is really more. We can all benefit if we consume less. Of course the idea will take longer to flower in some places than others. I used to be a pessimist, but now I am an optimist and believe things will improve… I have faith in people.

ABOVE A clean palette is enlivened by silver details. Here an elegant chaise invites ready lounging.

OPPOSITE Jaime Hayon's Showtime chairs contrast between classicism and modernity, and reflect off a polished Thassos floor. A faux rhino head serves as wall decoration.

OVERLEAF LEFT Yellow is used to vibrant effect in an otherwise white interior and black flocked decoy crows perch on the shelves. The ceiling is decorated with a transfer motif.

OVERLEAF RIGHT The only colour introduced is via the books on the shelves, while an Andromeda chandelier is the room's centrepiece.

A giant Archimoon light by
Philippe Starck and a wall-size portrait provides
dramatic focus in a room where the view is equally
extraordinary. A chaise longue is accompanied by
Asiatides and Bonze stools for further seating, and
viewing, options.

Here an unconventional use
of wall treatment challenges perspective.

ABOVE AND RIGHT Clean frameless mirrors, edged in pale yellow, and white Thassos tiles are essential details in the Minimal palette. Accessories include Romeo Babe Moon lights, Duravit vessel basins and Hansgrohe taps.

OPPOSITE A simply furnished bedroom is enhanced by the use of two delicate wall sconces by Kensington Lighting.

ARCHITECTURAL.

material
clean
geometric
spacious
cool
white
technical
industrial
minimal
blue

WANDERS & **yoo**

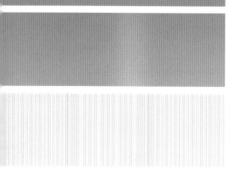

ARCHITECTURAL

With the Architectural palette, Marcel Wanders strips away the detail, the colour and the vibrancy that is usually associated with his work, and replaces it with a cool, clean look inspired by the big white spaces of modernism. "It's our way of looking at space and using it in a cleaner way," Wanders explains. "It is a language that plays more with the space than it does with the detailing. It's about using basic shapes and lines."

The keywords of the Architectural palette point to this pared-down approach: material, clean, geometric, spacious, cool, white, technical, industrial, minimal and blue. Many of these words are not usually associated with Wanders' work, but he is keen to point out that he is not turning into a purveyor of white boxes. "Don't think that Architectural means completely minimal!" he exclaims. "We won't just create boring white spaces. We will get the best out of spaces, create something dramatic out of them, instead of just leaving them as they are."

Rather than taking on the role of the architect, the Architectural palette offers interior designers a variety of ways of responding to existing interior spaces within the buildings that Wanders works on with Yoo. "We are not going to play the architect; we are going to work with architectural space. Sometimes we will have a building that is fabulous, and sometimes we will have a building that is not so incredible, but you know, there is always a sense of size, a sense of scale, there is a sense of definition of space."

The aim is to make spaces that are quieter, simpler, less detailed and emptier than the other palettes, even though they may contain many of the same fixtures and furnishings. "It leaves the architecture unharmed, and it draws you to understand its true quality. So you start understanding the building, the architectural space, the best way. So we will make a design that supports the individual qualities of the space. It could be a more intimate design that is more detailed; it could reinforce the volumes or it could blend with the volumes. You can make the shape of a space clearer, or you can blow it away."

Using space and light to create mood

Accepting and responding to the given architectural nature of the space is key to the Architectural palette. The critical decisions involve deciding how to alter the way natural light enters the space; developing a lighting strategy; and placing objects in the spaces. "It is these kinds of decisions that make an interior Architectural or not," Wanders explains. "You can put a cabinet against the wall, or you put it in the middle of space – it really makes space feel different. How you deal with the windows? Are you going to have transparent curtains, will they be very open, or very airy, or will they be dark velvet curtains?"

Lighting is also essential to creating a calm, airy mood, and unifying large spaces so they can be read as complete volumes. This palette uses more light than the others,

ABOVE Primarily neutral, the Architectural palette is cool and clean with a touch of blue. It incorporates embossed wallcoverings, white high-gloss lacquer and neutral wallpapers with aluminium blinds or sheer curtains for windows. Black wood, polyurethane and grey tartan carpeting or tiles provide flooring and Bisazza tiles and frameless mirrors are used in bathrooms.

OPPOSITE TOP The red outdoor cabana in the pool area of the Mondrian South Beach hotel features custom-made curtains, red patterned upholstered chairs, pillows and lights.

OPPOSITE For the Poliform "house of dreams", Wanders designed a space that features clean fabric wall coverings, white glossy floors and a signature warm red Artus sofa.

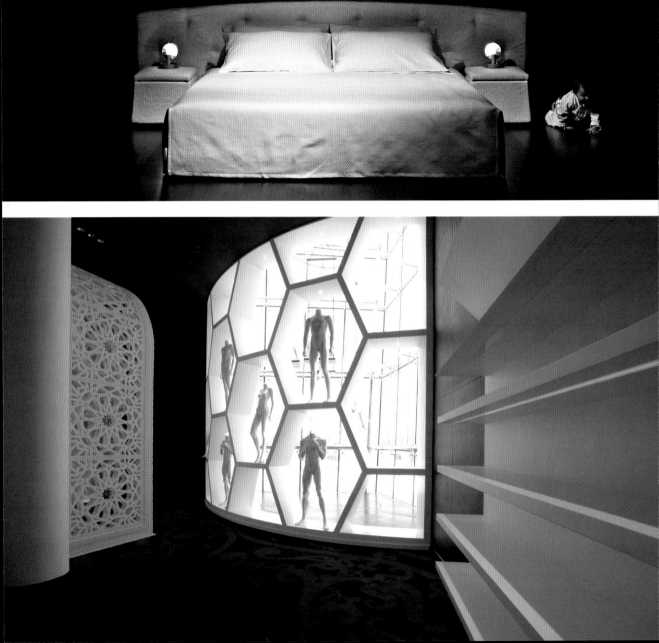

and the light works to highlight the architecture rather than the elements placed in the room. "The Architectural lighting will reinforce the shape of the architecture, the walls, the lines in the building," Wanders explains. "There will be more light. If you are in one corner you will be able to see the complete room, because I think it is important to get this kind of architectural understanding of space."

The materials that are selected for possible use in Architectural interiors include black wood and high-gloss white surfaces, stainless steel light switches and door furniture, aluminium blinds and white porcelain and chrome bathroom fittings. Overall the colour palette is muted, with blacks, whites and greys, plus metal finishes, although Wanders also suggests that blue is also a key colour in Architectural schemes. Floors are uncarpeted, with wood or polyurethane in the living areas and bedrooms and Bisazza mosaic tiling in the bathrooms.

While Wanders is best known for his expressive and playful approach to design, he says that an architectural approach has started to inform his studio as they take on more interior projects. "A lot of our projects have architectural definition; we make a lot of objects that are very architectural," he says, citing Sky Garden, a ceiling lamp that was designed in 2007 for the Italian brand Flos. Sleekly minimal and matt black on the outside, the white inside of the lamp features a subtle, floral bas-relief taken from the ceiling of an apartment that Wanders used to own in Amsterdam. This architectural detail is picked out and given definition by the light source. Wanders also cites Stone, a stool he designed for Kartell, as another product that encapsulates the Architectural approach. This is a translucent moulded plastic product with a facetted surface that resembles the surface of a cut jewel.

According to Wanders, the interiors project that most closely resembles how the Architectural palette works is Villa Moda, a store he completed in 2008 in Bahrain. Designed for the Villa Moda fashion and lifestyle chain, owned by Sheikh Majed of Kuwait, Wanders' interior design uses lighting, architecturally scaled elements and decorative screens to give definition to the store's vast expanse of space. Here too, black and white and grey are used extensively throughout, with occasional touches of gold and blue, while patterns, both floral and Islamic-inspired, are used on surfaces. The use of Islamic patterns on the screens at this store suggests how local architectural influences might be employed at properties around the world.

> The Architectural lighting will reinforce the shape of the architecture… If you are in one corner you will be able to see the complete room, because I think that is important to get that kind of architectural understanding of space.

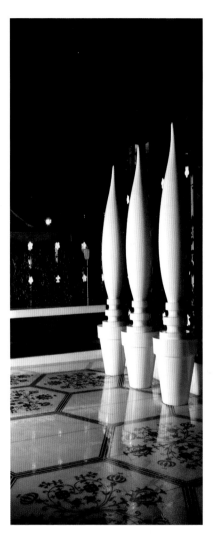

ABOVE In the garden of Villa Amsterdam, black-and-white, laser-cut, marble flooring and glossy, white topiaries form strong, geometric lines.

OPPOSITE TOP In this bedroom, an intense pure white highlights the distinctive pieces against a black backdrop, while a sculptural gold moose head sculpture, from Marcel Wanders' Personal Editions, lends dramatic effect.

OPPOSITE Wanders' design for the fashion store Villa Moda in Bahrain was inspired by the idea of a souk. Influences such as circular domes and stylized repeating decorative patterns from Islamic architecture can be seen in the latticeworked walls and digitally printed carpets.

MARCEL WANDERS

ABOVE Wanders' seminal piece, the Knotted chair from 1995. Designed for Droog and made of carbon and epoxy-coated aramid fibres, it is an adaptation of macramé, and his first piece to gain international recognition. The piece is lightweight and intricate yet strong and durable.

What is your approach to interior design?

With interior design we try to create spaces of surprise; to invite people and make them feel welcome in a place which is new to them and makes them feel different and excited.

How did your career as a designer begin?

Success came pretty fast in the design world. The Knotted Chair (1995) was an important breakthrough for me on the international scene. This became a sort of icon for my design and it immediately got us work all over the world. I was running my studio and we were doing a lot of projects – mostly product design to start with. We were designing in a very straightforward and direct way.

Gradually we started to do more and more interior design, beginning with the Expo 2000 in Hanover, Germany. We didn't really plan to start doing interiors; all of a sudden we had all these interior projects. But it felt like a logical step because it allowed us to surround people with our design, rather than just putting products in front of them.

What are the key interiors you've designed?

The first important interior design we did was Lute Suites, which is a row of converted eighteenth-century workers' cottages besides the River Amstel at Ouderkerk near Amsterdam, that we converted into a series of seven guest suites in 2005. Lute Suites function like a cross between a hotel and holiday cottages. This was our first design that relates to hospitality, to the home. So it addressed a larger audience.

The next big step for us was working on Mondrian South Beach, a hotel and apartment complex on Miami Beach. This was our first large-scale interior project. It opened a few months ago. There we have created a magical world based around the idea of "Sleeping Beauty's castle", with a spectacular interior and gardens like an oasis with indoor/outdoor spaces, a chandelier hanging above the pool, cabanas and tented play spaces for children. The curved building has rooms resembling theatrical boxes overlooking the gardens below, so that everyone has the best seat in the house. And the next big step for us is working with Yoo. This is a new level for us and we are very excited.

What are the main differences in the way you approach interior design and product design?

When we design interiors it is completely different from when we design products. As product designers we pursue an idea in a concrete way and you know that at the end of the process there is the product. This is like a sculptor who has a piece of marble and keeps chipping away until by the time he is done everything is perfect.

And the way we work on interiors is completely different because with an interior, if you define a single idea straight away, it's very boring; it's dead almost. We design them far more so that people find their own ways to make use of them. It's like making a magazine; we have a thousand different ideas and we make them work together so that, you know, you can move through it.

Unlike product design, interiors are about theatre, leading you from one idea to the next and the next. You need to breathe life into a space. You want people to go from one feeling into another feeling. So an interior is about the travelling, it's a journey more than it is an object. It's a moment, it's a time frame.

How do you balance function and style in an interior?

There are a lot of interiors where function is essential and we all use them everyday and don't really notice them. But there are other cases where, if you are in a space, you really want to know you are in it. In these cases we really want to create the most fabulous thing we could imagine. And then of course you can inject more drama and theatricality.

A hotel, for example, is used by a lot of different people – they go there for entertainment, they go there for some functionality also, but it's really a place to hang out and have fun.

How do you use colour?

Most of the time colour is a way for us to decorate things. Black and white are the two basic colours that are essential to us. We love to be clear and direct and to contrast these colours in the work. We also use a lot of colours like gold, silver and brown, which are colours that for me create a sense of space in a very natural, basic way. Then sometimes we use a more dramatic or surprising colour, something we would never normally use, like a minty green or a crazy yellow, in order to pick up on something.

How much does Dutch design, culture and landscape influence your work?

When I started I would have been irritated by this question. But more and more, I understand it in a different way. I think design is like making gifts for people; that's why I like it so much. When you give someone a gift, you just don't give anything; you give something that resonates with who they are. That makes it a good gift. The other quality of a good gift is that it should not be something this person could get from anyone. So if you are a designer you should give your audience things you want to give, things that resonate with them and things that are about you.

Finally, tell us a little about the four themes you have developed for Yoo.

We came up with these four words – architectural, eclectic, new antiques and natural. These are four directions and each has its own space, but also they are to be used together. So if we do a hotel for example, one area could be one theme and the next area another… we will give people choices in these four directions.

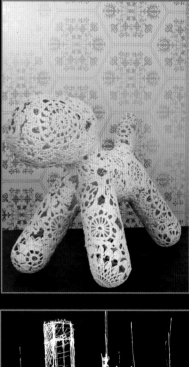

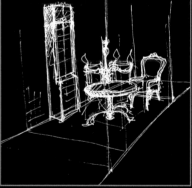

TOP Marcel Wanders has created custom pieces and ranges for clients including Bisazza, Boffi, Cappellini, Colorline, Flos and Vitra. Pictured here is the yellow Stella wallpaper from the Graham & Brown Couture collection and the Crochet Puppy from Marcel Wanders' Personal Editions.

ABOVE A sketch of the reception at Lute Suites.

ARISTO.

damask
leather car seats
papa's old jag
duck-egg blue
bryan ferry
marble
whisky and water
lamplight
savile row suit linings
persian

JADE JAGGER for **yoo**

ARISTO

A shared sense of history inspired the palette for Aristo. Jade Jagger and Tom Bartlett both have a deep knowledge of and affection for the English countryside, and so picked it as their starting point. "It made us think of National Trust houses, lush fields, coming in from rainy country walks, discovering an old ruined building, tea with granny at the Ritz," says Bartlett. "Which led us to our colour scheme," adds Jagger. "Duck-egg blue, leather brown, sage green, verdigris, lime white. Historic colours are integral to the scheme. The palette had to include those faded hues that work so well in weak northern light. For us, it represented a unifying, familiar and comfortable childhood place. Those colours, of course, led onto the materials that are often used in that kind of grand building. We found ourselves drawn to rich leather, damask, stone, velvet, corduroy and gun metal."

Of course, this is tradition with a twist. "It's more a nod towards the eccentricity of the English, looking back over our unique architectural history," says Bartlett. Their project together for the reinvention of the crown jewellers Garrard, where Jade was creative director, gave the team a reference point. "Because we have worked together for so long, we knew instinctively what we wanted," observes Jagger. "We looked back at the work we had done on the store concepts, which were very much around heritage, traditional materials and a very deep-rooted British sensibility."

Jagger and Bartlett wanted to create an environment that personified a self-assured, comfortable and wise soul. "It's not shouting," explains Bartlett. "In that way of a sage, older person we wanted it to feel calmer, but quite forceful, creating a feeling of safety and stability."

"I used to live in the English countryside in an estate farm house," says Jagger, "and for me it is all about the heaviness and brocade of the fabrics and that kind of 'khakiness', and that light drifts into those big old houses. It is very romantic, but also has a real sense of consistency and calm, which is as much about the landscape as it is the people." Although in theory each of the schemes can be applied, in some format, to any property, of all of the concepts, this one seems most naturally to represent a sense of family, Englishness and permanence. "This scheme is very much for a home, not just a house," says Jagger.

Modern sophistication

Creating a modern home with a sense of history is a delicate balance. "It is simply finding the right balance," says Bartlett. "A mix of old and new is always interesting, as they provide a foil for one another. Of course, the two main ways to do it are to take a decorative line in a very contemporary space or to take an historic interior and juxtapose it with modern pieces." This can of course can be applied on a smaller level," adds Jagger. "By taking an old chair and lacquering it you can turn it into something else completely."

ABOVE Historical colours and materials make up the Aristo palette, including lime white, duck-egg blue, sage and vertis green shades, as well as traditional tiling, leather, damask, wood panelling and black veined marble to ground the scheme.

OPPOSITE A dining space that can be casual and transform into a formal setting is central to the Aristo concept. High gloss floors reflect, in this instance, the Lakes setting. Furniture brings a contemporary freshness to a formal dining arrangement, and keeps the look modern and sophisticated rather than too traditional.

With this in mind, iconic British classic pieces such as the Aga cooker have been reinvented with bold coloured finishes. As well being physically warm, the bold Aga creates a visual centerpiece. "The kitchen is very important. At least it is in my own home," says Jagger. "We have an Aga, and I love the weightiness and solidity of it, and the fact that it is the non-stop heart of the home. It's the warmth and the cosiness that creates a sense of a real family space."

From the its inception, the Aristo palette was intended to appeal to families and their specific needs. "It made us want to create that sense of acceptance and intimacy of a family. So, we knew we wanted it to be able to translate into any space and it would still have a proper kitchen, even if, due to an apartment's size, it was just a small one," says Jagger. Bartlett continues, "Fireplaces or kitchens give a sense of a family-friendly space, a relaxing place where generations can gather around a hearth; a place to which a person can 'come home'." The pair have reinforced this ease with comforting materials such as rich leather. Of course, rather than using it simply on a chair, they suggests a leather floor or fire surround. "It's the smell!" says Jagger, "it's just so incredibly evocative."

When using so many classical or traditional references, it is important not to slide into parody. Jagger explains, "If you are using traditional pieces, like a leather Chesterfield, they work best when used with simplicity. It's really important that you don't let things get over-cluttered, or the whole space can look like it's falling down!" Jagger suggests simplifying a period house, with details such as cornicing or pillars, and neutralizing the detailing with white so that the shapes add interest rather than over-power. "Using white can turn any interior into a clean modern background, so that you can have contrast."

Jagger reinforces however, that before the surface decoration is applied, the way in which you live needs to be considered. "It is really important to find the flow of the space," says Jagger. "A space should accommodate how you like to live. You need to feel comfortable in it, and part of that is the way it responds well to your needs." Naturally, this includes flexibility. Jagger extrapolates, "You need to consider things like how it works when you want to kick back and watch TV, if the space can be opened up for gatherings, or closed off to make it more intimate." Bartlett adds, "We hate dead space, and we want what you do have to really reflect your idea of the home. So would you like to create a picture window so you can look out at the view from your bed, or a calming en suite bedroom? The space should help you get more out of your everyday, and enrich your quality of life."

The kitchen is very important. . . we have an Aga, and I love the weightiness and solidity of it and the fact that it is the non-stop heart of the home.

OPPOSITE TOP The bold colour of the Aga gives a beloved classic contemporary relevance and serves as a focal point in the kitchen–dining area. Furniture includes mid-century classics – an Eero Saarinen Tulip dining table accompanied by Eames chairs.

OPPOSITE Soft ambient lighting helps promote the idea of the traditional after-dinner estate smoking room, while striped upholstery gives the room a masculine edge. A Lama leather chaise longue by Zanotta is shown on the left and a Spun floor lamp by Sebastian Wong appears far right.

TOP AND CENTRE Artfully placed Garrard silver recalls an aristocratic golden age and lends an elegant burnished glow to the decorating scheme.

ABOVE John Hitchcox, Tom Bartlett and Jade Jagger collaborating on design plans.

LEFT Brick-style white subway tiles line a spacious bathroom. Back-painted pink glass on the mirror lends colour to a black-and-white decor that includes a ceramic mosaic-tiled floor. A Thonet bentwood chair and Tod table in white varnished polypropylene by Zanotta appear on the right.

TOP AND ABOVE Elegance is in the details. Classic tap fixtures by Lefroy Brooks are set in a mirrored splashback while a marble bathroom is softened by the use of delicate voile curtains and a traditional roll-top claw-foot bath by CP Hart.

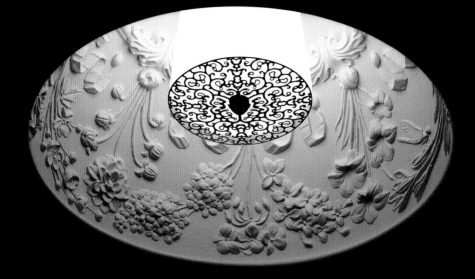
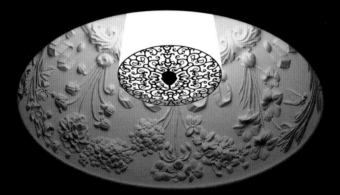
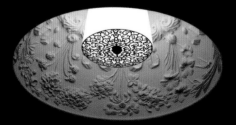
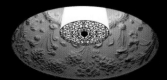

NEW ANTIQUES.

contrasts of past and future
sophisticated
cultural
black and white

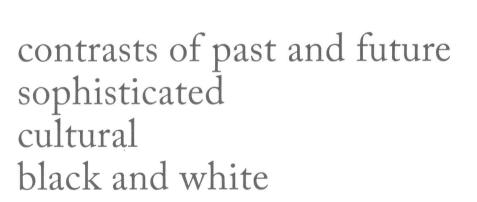

WANDERS & **yoo**

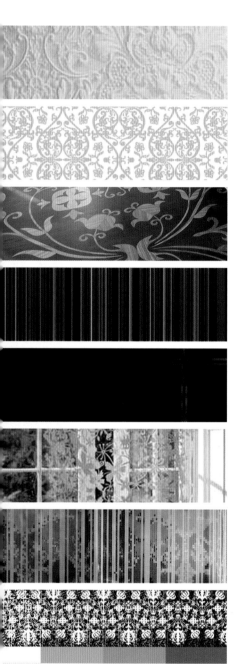

NEW ANTIQUES

Why are avant-garde designers so obsessed with the future? Why does an interior have to pretend the past never existed? These are the questions that Marcel Wanders attempts to answer with his New Antiques palette; an approach to design that takes the forms and themes of the past and re-evaluates them for contemporary living. "The design world thinks that there is only a future, there is not a history, there is not a past," explains Wanders. "The whole philosophy of New Antiques goes back to before modernism. The least we can do is to skip this period and go back to the moment where we lost our past, and to start from there."

One of the key phrases for the New Antiques palette is "contrasts of past and future", and a New Antiques interior might typically feature a mixture of both contemporary and antique furniture and objects, placed together to create unusual juxtapositions. This creates a sense of continuity with the past instead of a clean break from it, which is what many other contemporary designers aim to achieve.

Wanders has already used this technique of mixing old and new in some of his furniture designs, such as his series of tables and chairs made of traditional lace. These designs, called Lace tables and Crochet chairs, are constructed of hand-made white lace flowers that are produced by skilled craftswomen in the time-honoured way. The fabric is then strengthened with epoxy resin and moulded over a form to create a solid, unsupported form. Thus an old-fashioned material is given a dramatic and contemporary twist. This approach is also seen in the Paris mirror, created for Quodes (see page 43), which recollects an ornate eighteenth-century boudoir mirror, as well as the domed Skygarden lamp (see page 74) with plasterwork detailing on the inside and a liquid paint finish, which was based on a traditional plasterwork ceiling motif.

Both the name and the concept of the New Antiques palette comes from a range of furniture that Wanders designed for Cappellini, the leading Italian design brand, in 2005. Based on traditional, Italian, turned-wood furniture, the range features dark wood chairs with leather seats that are tooled with decorative patterns, and occasional tables with spindly turned legs and smoked glass tops. These pieces make no attempt to be faithful reproductions of old furniture, nor were they a banal restyling exercise; instead, they take the spirit of a familiar form and re-imagine it for today.

New Antiques is not nostalgic. It does not attempt to recreate historic interiors. Rather, it takes what Wanders calls "the opulence of form", which resides in certain familiar items from the past, and exaggerates it's formal characteristics so that it becomes new. "New Antiques is not a study of history, we never work with antique pieces as such," Wanders explains. "It's more like the idea of history, used as a reference for a design that is in the future and in the past. And so, in a way, New Antiques is completely strange; we try to use a certain sophisticated sensibility."

ABOVE An ornate palette that re-imagines historical and heritage elements, New Antiques includes wenge wood, parquet, black wood and polyurethane flooring, as well as embossed wallcoverings and white and black high-gloss paint. Ausbrenner or sheer curtains are used for windows, with white Bardelli ceramic relief tiles and Bisazza tiles for bathrooms.

OPPOSITE TOP AND BOTTOM Over-scaled columns with ornate profiles, suggestive of an ancient temple or classical ruin, appear in Wanders' public areas for the Mondrian South Beach hotel in Miami Beach. In the dining area, golden candelabras appear in table-size and in giant proportions, rethinking the traditional lighting accessory, while the gold and yellow carpet enriches the setting.

Black and white

The key colour combination used throughout New Antiques, both for the furnishings and the interiors themselves, is black and white. Wanders explains that the use of black and white allows the designers to extract form and emotion from historic typologies, while presenting them as something new and free of sentimentality. "If you see an antique piece, you want to see it today," explains Wanders. "You want to bring something to it so it feels like it's new and different. The use of black and white becomes the way to do it. It becomes stronger, the form becomes more formal and the decoration starts to be a little bit softer. It's our way to digest the opulence of form." The Lace tables and Crochet chairs, and the New Antiques furniture for Cappellini, are all produced in monochrome black or white for these reasons.

Black and white – or darkness and light – is a key feature of the lighting approach to the New Antiques palette. Instead of uniform lighting, parts of the interiors are picked out with light while other areas are more shadowy. "In the New Antiques areas the light could be more specific," says Wanders. "There would be dark areas, there would be light areas, depending on the mood."

Mood boards for the New Antiques interiors suggest the use of wenge wood and polyurethane floor finishes. They also include many of Wanders' own designs for fixtures and fittings, including the Aqua Jewels range of brassware, for Italian company Bonomi, for the bathrooms. Bedrooms are carpeted in a range that Wanders designed for the Dutch company Colorline. Called World Carpets, this range allows purchasers to choose from a variety of different patterns that are combined at the factory to produce unique designs. These uniquely patterned carpets, along with custom-designed wooden parquet flooring that typically features in the New Antiques theme, creates an atmosphere that reflects past and present.

New Antiques… is more like the idea of history, used as a reference for a design that is in the future and in the past. And so, in a way, New Antiques is completely strange…

OPPOSITE Everything in this room at Villa Amsterdam is custom made, from the patterned plaster ceiling and the inlaid parquet floor, to the chaise longue covered in Marcel Wanders' signature Jester fabric, featuring his clown face.

RIGHT TOP AND BOTTOM Marcel Wanders' Personal Editions exhibition in Milan 2007 showed antique furniture coated in classic grey featuring One Minute Delftware and One Minute Sculptures, exhibited on custom Colorline carpets.

CLASSIC.

cigar
jaguar
labrador
english club
familiar
tailored
reassuring
connolly leather
library
silk
tweed
aston martin
marble
horses

yoo inspired by STARCK

CLASSIC

"Our Classic style is what you might expect… here is a home filled with objects that are well crafted and carefully chosen," says Philippe Starck. The evolution of this palette began with the pursuit of old-fashioned excellence in design, materials and craftsmanship. It is a very comfortable and familiar palette, replete with objects and finishes that have a timeless quality because they are beautifully designed and tailor made. This is a far cry from the speed, excesses and instant gratification that characterizes many aspects of modern life. This is about the pleasures of taking things slowly and revelling in the process of careful consideration.

The Classic concept sits well with Starck's philosophy of moving away from our rapacious appetite for excess. "We need fewer possessions in our lives, and those items that we do own must be better made than before. They must be long lasting," he proposes. "We can use our huge knowledge of design and technology to make the best and most economic use of materials. We should promote built-in longevity because this makes a lot more sense than recycling."

Starck has a clear image of the type of person who would appreciate the Classic lifestyle. "The person who finds this palette most appealing is a connoisseur. Here is someone who understands and enjoys the finer things in life. It is deeply tactile and sensual, appealing to all the senses. We could be talking about soft leather, with that wonderful leathery polished smell, or the aroma of leather-bound books, dark wood, like the sort of thing you might find on the dashboard of a classic car or beautiful boat, lots of mahogany. This could be a middle-aged man who loves the feel of cashmere, the smell of cigar smoke, Mozart and objects that are timeless and good. We are talking about shoes by Lobb, an Hermès belt, a Land Rover or Jaguar." But equally, this could appeal to a woman who lives an urban life, is extremely sophisticated, and knows how to mix some of the classic elements with contemporary objects. Of course, there is an element of elitism: when people work hard and have a particular sensibility, they can afford to indulge themselves.

The broad mix of materials involved in this palette is a reflection of those used in much of Starck's famous design work. The aluminium that he has used in a number of his design projects, including the iconic and spidery Juicy Salif lemon squeezer; the rich woods he uses in his furniture, including his famous Café Costes chair; and the gleaming metals that have also been sculpted for his fantastic motorbike designs, including those for Aprilia.

Creating style with substance

As with all projects where Starck is involved, whether it is a restaurant, a bar or a home, the very special quality of the place begins with the quality of the space. "The starting point of any home has to be the space and we work extremely hard on the plan of every apartment," says Starck. "We do follow some rules, and the first

ABOVE Pale grey and white are combined within the Classic palette. Limestone, merbau, walnut and sisal provide flooring options and polished chrome is used for finishes and fixtures.

OPPOSITE An extra-long 9m (30ft) reception table and chandelier were custom-made for this lobby in the Icon South Beach.

ABOVE Sculptor, Jocelyn Bocquine, first made a clay maquette of the horse, which was cast in ceramic before being sent out to Dubai to be copied in pure white porcelain in the form of a unicorn.

ABOVE The Classic palette relies on a connection to mythologies and ancient history. This image – *The Cock Fight* by Jean-Léon Gérôme – has been used as a wall treatment and as inspiration for the palette.

OPPOSITE When developing the G-Tower concept in Dubai, the Yoo team first decided on a white horse to grace the lobby – which combined two lucky symbols in the Middle East, the horse and the colour white. For a mythical connection, Starck decided to make the leap to the unicorn, lining them up like Trojan horses in the 10m- (33ft-) high room. Over-scaled themselves, at 7m (23ft) high, they stand on a marble floor with outsized geometric patterning. The entire effect is carefully constructed in order to create a feeling of immensity.

is that every home must be noble and 'aristocratic' in volume. This doesn't mean it has to be huge, even the smallest rooms become superior when they are based on good proportions." While Starck's space-engineering skills are clearly evident in his handling of huge areas, at his famous hotels and restaurants – for example the glamorous Royalton in New York, sexy Hotel Fasano in Rio de Janeiro and the amazing Peninsula Hotel Restaurant in Hong Kong – every visitor should take time to explore the bathrooms or lavatories to see that he is also a maestro of the miniature. In even the smallest rooms there is room for the drama of a theatrical curtain, an exotic fabric or an oversized piece of furniture.

While the quest for pleasing proportions is relatively straightforward in new buildings, the true challenge comes in dealing with conversions of existing structures. The process of transformation from an old factory, an office or warehouse to a home is complex because the old building must be shaped and moulded into a place for living in. When converting existing buildings, full consideration is given to the creation of symmetrical and balanced spaces. "We are always looking for good proportions," says Starck. "They are healthy and quiet and simple. For me, symmetrical architecture is very pleasing. On the other hand, it can be very stressful, especially in a building that is a renovation, to see spaces cut up in strange ways with one window up high and another stuck down by the floor. Even when an apartment is small, it must always have good proportions."

The route to revealing those good proportions is to strip away all extraneous layers and details and go back to the walls, to the very bones of the structure. This is true when setting out to make the most of any home. With a place stripped bare, it becomes easier to see and understand what you are dealing with and it is possible to start creating great proportions and volumes.

With its emphasis on sensuality, the Classic palette is restrained in terms of colours and doesn't veer far from pale neutrals and a range of dark browns; but it incorporates exquisite textures, including cool marble, warm woods and chunky fabrics. Far from being limited, this restraint can produce interiors with tremendous coherence. This might include a bathroom lined entirely in creamy-coloured limestone or marble to ensure that the emphasis is on calmness and purity, or it might be a bathroom lined with rich wood, perhaps a teak or mahogany, which creates a great sense of luxury, reminiscent of a gentleman's club or the smartest yacht.

However, there is room for more exuberance too. The carefully controlled Classic backdrop sets the stage for wonderful surprises, perhaps a shimmering, oversize chandelier or a man-sized Anglepoise lamp, a vast mirror; or a line-up of gleaming, white, model unicorns, each one the size of a house. In the same way that the most exquisitely tailored suit can appear plain and simple at first glance, close attention to the detail will reveal surprise and delight. For example, the plain suit might be unbuttoned to reveal a waistcoat embellished with richly coloured silk embroidery and gleaming pearly buttons.

The secret of enjoying the Classic palette is to use the senses of a connoisseur… take in the aromas of timber and leather, run your fingers across the cool marble and the warm, finely woven fabrics and feast your eyes on the superb craftsmanship of gorgeous finishes.

OPPOSITE An Andromeda chandelier and custom-made mirror by Thomas Tisch appears in this entrance. Standard-issue US mailboxes in gold line the walls on the left.

TOP A small gathering of chairs includes an African bead market-find and an Emeco chair. The Venetian mirror is by Fratelli Barbini.

ABOVE Floor-standing Pols Potten vases appear in a setting inspired by the films of David Lynch.

ABOVE A Classic palette provides an ideal backdrop for surprising elements, such as the giant Anglepoise lamp, here being adjusted by Philippe Starck.

OPPOSITE A grey cashmere Hermès blanket adorns a Neoz bed by Philippe Starck for Driade. The merbau blinds give warmth in a neutrally decorated bedroom.

OPPOSITE Merbau wood is used to give a club-like warmth to a bathroom, via the timber basin stand and mirror frame. The floors are French limestone and the lights are Romeo Babe.

ABOVE The favourite of shipbuilders since the Middle Ages, teak has durability and flexibility, and provides a rustic elegance when used lavishly in a bathroom.

The person who finds this palette most appealing is a connoisseur. Here is someone who understands and enjoys the finer things in life…

CLUB.

eclectic
timber
e-type
ottoman
leather
bespoke
engraved
whisky
ochre
velvet
chesterfield
jazz

yoo design studio

Using a warm, masculine theme, the Club palette offers grey velvet, brown leather upholstery and American walnut flooring. It incorporates yellow ochre, velvet curtains, gold leaf, burnished metal, decorative graphics and Empress marble.

CLUB

Mark Davison of Yoo Design Studio is quick to point out that the Club palette is not "club, as in Ibiza club", but is more like something that you might find in an old fashioned, St James's gentlemen's club – comfortable and slightly old worldy, with a strong sense of tradition and history. Its hallmarks are relaxed surroundings, warmth and soft edges, bound by a certain element of heritage. "In the face of the transience of our throwaway culture, Club has a sense of solidity about it, and certain people are very attracted to that," says Davison. Club is about fireplaces and comfortable sofas, although it doesn't need a grand, massively proportioned interior for it to work well. "There are no plastic finishes in the palette," adds Julieann Humphryes, who oversees the detailed development of the studio's palette of styles. "Club is about attention to detail and materials that have a certain patina, quality and longevity to them."

The combination of historical features and contemporary details is an important aspect of the Club palette. How light enters the room also adds depth to the space. According to Humphryes, this is best achieved with very simple, unfussy Venetian blinds in wood or metal. "Either that or a plain, sheer curtain. Something very fine in cotton or another semitransparent fabric," she says. How the studio actually fits the curtain is also critical. "It's always something that's simply folded or pleated," explains Humphryes, "and we try to hide the mechanics of it if we can, which isn't always easy. A big recess in the ceiling works – the Americans call it a 'curtain trough'. These are the details that just set the stage beautifully for someone to come in and create their own space, because they are not then fighting with what's already there."

Part of Yoo Design Studio's current approach is also reducing the amount of technology that is visible and out on display. According to Davison, dimming the lights by remote control or having a giant television screen rise out of the end of the bed is slightly playboyish: "We've done it, all of it," he says, "but it's not where we want to go any more." The approach that is now being used is far more about subtly introducing elements of technology into the home, and working them around more important factors, such as enjoying space, light and the view. "We try really hard to say to people that actually it's really nice not to have a TV in your bedroom," explains Davison. "Make a bedroom about sleeping, lovemaking, whatever, instead. We will still put TV points in the master bedroom, of course, but we always make the bed face the view, the window. Developers might come back to us and say, 'Yes, but how can you see the TV, where will the TV go?', and we say, 'The TV can go here, you can swing it out if you need to, or it can be concealed in a cupboard.'"

Working with historical features

Maintaining as much historical architectural detail in a building as they can is also important to Yoo Design Studio. "If it was something that was great, but multicoloured, we might blitz it with warm grey paint and reduce it to a weird, but historical, backdrop," reveals Humphryes, "and if it was egg-and-dart cornicing, but traditionally a sort of duck egg blue, we wouldn't stay with the duck egg blue – we'd keep the form not necessarily the finish." The studio considers these to be the kind of details that ultimately add to the character of a space. "We don't conceal historical, architectural quirks," concurs Davison, "not even in an industrial building, which is something that goes right back to our beginnings with Manhattan Loft Corporation. Our view is, let's try and draw as much character out of these places as we can."

The studio may have taken their inspiration for Club from the deep, rich tones of the traditional, gentleman's private club, but they offset this with ornate flashes of gold, decorative mirrors and mustard tones that are introduced through paint or fabrics. These colourful and eclectic introductions lift the palette, and reinvent what might otherwise be seen as a mere pastiche of an historic style. Silk carpets, for example, are used to imply that the owner of the property is well travelled, and also add to the luxurious sheen of the surrounding materials. The rugs appear as more of a detail, subtly thrown down on the floor in the bedroom area to add warmth. Meanwhile, American walnut provides the right rich and intense finish for flooring in the Club palette, while "polished dark brown marble is matched with wooden cabinetry," notes Davison. "The contrast of wood with this very shiny surface, with a white vein running through it, is incredibly luxurious."

The mustard wall colourings might seem experimental to some, but as Humphryes explains, they "work brilliantly to balance the gold details on objects and lamps". Spotlights are studiously avoided in favour of handsome, old anglepoise table lamps, or perhaps more lavish table lamps with gilded or glass decorative details. Other furnishings are eclectic vintage or collected items, for example a beautiful old leather Chesterfield might appear alongside a more modern piece. "We definitely introduce leather and velvets in upholstery, and these can even be slightly worn in and used," continues Humphryes. "Having said that, a perfectly buttoned, shiny leather Chesterfield really anchors the room – it's a large, bold statement object."

One of the elements that is particularly pertinent to the Club palette is the inclusion of a fireplace. "We love the fireplace," enthuses Davison. "Every time we can, we include one, even in some of the craziest countries, like Singapore or Miami – it's more the idea of it than the practical application." According to Davison, a fireplace is a given for a living area because it focuses a room. As you walk into a space the first thing you see should be the fireplace, not the television. "Having said that, some people stick the TV directly above the fireplace," admits Davison, "and that's really not what we do either. If you're sitting on the sofa, the centre of the TV should be at eye-level, otherwise you've got the 'first row of the cinema' sort of problem. So put it in a cupboard by the side of the fireplace, or whatever, just not above it."

Gel fires are far better than they used to be, but there is nothing like a proper wood-burning fire, or at least a real-flame gas fire. "A fireplace makes a home a home, and gives warmth in any space – we often have fireplaces in the lobby of a building," says Davison. "We'll have big, soft sofas surrounding it and everybody just sighs as they come in, it's just really nice. A fireplace is a priority in my book."

We don't conceal historical, architectural quirks. . . . Our view is, let's try to draw as much character out of these places as we can.

TOP Elements of the traditional gentlemen's club – a library and billiard table – are reinvented with the use of bright crimson colour. Changing the scale of the wall images and the pendant lights adds to the internal drama.

ABOVE Vibrant shades such as orange, brown and blue pick up the warmth of the dark wood surface of the Moooi Container table (hand-painted brown) and the Jaime Hayon seating in custom colours.

TECHNO.

matt/shiny
black glass
suede
gimlet
sushi
the white stripes
sleek
tokyo
tamagotchi
iPod

JADE JAGGER for **yoo**

TECHNO

The Techno look distils the very essence of fast-paced metropolitan life. In fact, the Jade Jagger and Tom Bartlett team wanted to create a space that recalled the most desirable of ultra-modern hotel rooms. "We had ideas about black glass, very urban, very sleek, the best kind of high-rise living," says Bartlett. "We felt that this type of environment would appeal to someone who frequents the great cities of the world, and likes the finer things in life," says Jagger, continuing, "They would have an appreciation of well-made objects, like a fabulous watch or a beautiful sleek car." They also recognize that this style has a definitive gender bias. "It is a more masculine scheme," says Bartlett, "but it is essentially about modernity, which of course is an aesthetic both sexes appreciate."

When creating this scheme, Bartlett recalls the brash electronics and technology that is often associated with the classic bachelor pad. But rather than pack the space with soon-to-be obsolete gadgets, this idea was subverted into shiny surfaces and sharp fluorescent details. The overall effect is of a very energetic and dynamic environment. "Our inspiration here definitely had a nod to the 1980s," laughs Jagger, "but that was more about it having a sense of the very graphic and it is very linear. This is less about pattern adorning a surface and more about shapes." "There was also a touch of the Donald Judd about it," adds Bartlett, referring to the American sculptor who made his name with unequivocal solid forms. "That sense of a shiny box, something very definite and delineated."

The predominate colourways are red, black, white and silver, which are manifest in a myriad of hard-edged materials such as lacquer, Perspex, glass, chrome and resin. Lighting was also an essential part of creating the right atmosphere. The concealed lighting in the bathroom not only adds gloss that bounces back off the rimless shower enclosure and black mosaics, but also creates a sultry "city that never sleeps" feel. "Nondirect side lighting is great for giving a clear reflection and a flattering, sophisticated feel," says Bartlett, "and if the bathroom space is windowless, you can still make it feel special by giving the lighting plan some serious thought. We always like the bathroom to feel like a space that is very indulgent, because it's where most people spend time on themselves, where they get some space to think and relax."

Working with strong colours

"The key to working with bold hues is to make sure that you get the balance right," says Bartlett. He continues, "It is all about the quantity. For example, you can make a whole room red, and you will get the strength of the hit but not the full visual impact. It needs something to play off against." Too much pattern or too many textures are also overwhelming, so plain areas of colour are needed to provide relief and to give the eye a rest. As a guide, Jagger and Bartlett

ABOVE Shiny and sleek, the Techno colourway is mainly limited to red, orange, black and white. Blond flooring is used as a framework with highly slick, reflective materials – such as resin floors, gloss tiles, lacquer and Perspex.

OPPOSITE A vivid crimson-and-gold wallpaper is balanced by op-art black-and-white cushions. The juxtaposition of floral and geometric patterns works because of the rigorous use of a limited black, red and white palette.

There was a touch of the Donald Judd about it… that sense of a shiny box, something very definite and delineated.

advise using such hues in measured percentages. Jagger explains, "Before you start buying furniture or painting walls, consider the dominance of each colour. Proportionally we tend to apply 60 per cent white, 30 per cent black and 10 per cent red."

"Strong colours can unify and give personality to a room, but the skill lies in using them to effect without letting them dominate a scheme", comments Bartlett. "If you have a base scheme of black, white and silver with only one accent colour, you can use that accent to stunning effect. Just one red chair, or a clever detail can work. If you have a cut-out handle on a red kitchen cupboard door, it will trick the mind into assuming that the whole interior of the door is red, so it's impact becomes more forceful."

"But considering the proportional use of a vivid colour isn't enough," says Jagger. "The finishes used in this scheme are carefully selected to work specifically with the bold colours. A lacquered black or red finish will help subtly reduce its impact with the reflective surfaces." By the same token, offsetting a black wall or furniture against gently undulating sheer curtains accentuates the individual properties of both. The team also use discrete surface changes to keep the hit of any one colour from dominating. A bold red wallpaper with a florid gold pattern is prevented from overpowering the scheme through the careful placement of equally arresting black and white pillows.

There are, true to the Jagger and Bartlett style, twists using intense colours in this scheme that stop it from resting on its laurels. As well as the fitting Johnny B Good light by Ingo Maurer, which is as pared-back as any piece of design could be, and the seamless and lean Spun light by Sebastian Wong for Flos, the craft feel of the upholstery on the Zanotta sofa prevents the scheme from being too sleek and provides the perfect foil.

"Using such a piece against black is very effective," says Jagger. "I always use black in my own home, as it makes whatever you put in front of it really pop, creating a visual hit. It means you can play a lot with what you put in front of it. I also think that black is a very elegant colour, and it can be mixed well with most other hues and is a great foundation colour. If it doesn't work you can always paint over it!"

When it comes to strong hot colours such as orange, red or pink, Jagger suggests introducing them in soft furnishings such as a chair upholstery, throw or lampshade. "Although they are still vivid, it makes them easy to live with and gives them, literally as well as visually, a softer edge," she explains. The team do however, always favour an overall neutral palette against which to create focal points. The blond wood flooring and white walls that surround these more strident aspects work almost as a visual frame, at once giving shape to, and relief from, their intensity. The result is a much more fresh and organic take on the bachelor pad than the 1980s inspiration that sparked the Techno theme.

ABOVE The dominant colourway of black, white and red is carefully balanced to create a bold but still elegant scheme. A red splashback turns a functional kitchen space into something much more arresting. The lacquer gloss units were custom-made in Italy and hand-assembled on site.

OPPOSITE TOP A Zanotta sofa in a craft-inspired upholstery is the visual centrepiece of the room. The black lacquer Pod houses the bathroom and kitchen facilities and separates the living room from the dining area.

OPPOSITE BOTTOM Blond wood flooring and sheer window treatments add a luxurious contrast to harder-edged design pieces. Red Campari lights by Ingo Maurer are set over the Eero Saarinen Tulip table and New Antiques chairs by Marcel Wanders, while a floor-standing Lily lamp by Freedom of Creation is seen in the foreground.

ABOVE Within the bathroom, black is permitted to dominate. Walls are covered floor to ceiling with tiny mosaic tiles to provide a dramatic graphic effect that emphasizes the cube shape of the Pod. Concealed lighting behind the mirror creates a flattering glow and clear reflection.

OPPOSITE For the ultimate jet setter: the world in time zones. In a surrealist idea that requires minimal decorating skill (using simple masking tape and paint), a giant mustard yellow circle bridges the corner of a room and provides a designated work area.

CITY.

international
monochromatic
vespa
sharp
lustre
stainless
luxurious
reflective
vodka
edge-lit
mobile
metro
rsvp
sexy

yoo design studio

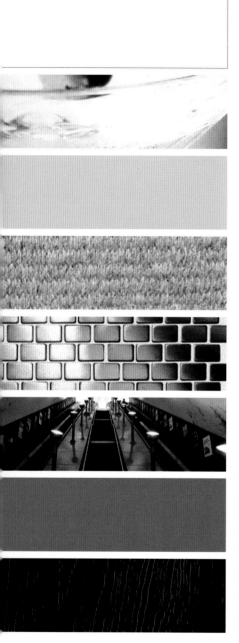

CITY

"When you're in the city, you're not just playing to the city, you've got to provide a refuge from it as well," explains Yoo Design Studio's Mark Davison. "A lot of cities, because of the climate and density of population, are actually quite tough places to live in. Your home is essentially an escape from that urban turmoil, but it's also a celebration of the city you love and live in, so you want to introduce a bit of that into your home." Having worked for many years creating the original and ultimate "City boys" loft apartments for Manhattan Loft Corporation, Davison came to Yoo with an intimate understanding of what does and does not work in urban spaces.

"Forget about the building," argues Davison, "the building can be anything on the outside, but when you are sitting in your own home on your sofa, or lying in your bed you want to make sure that the view is in the right place. That affects more people's lives than walking out and looking up, back at the building, and saying, 'Oh, isn't that a marvellous edifice that we live in.' Sure, how the building we live in looks on the outside is part of our life experience, but our real experience is all to do with what we can touch and feel, and how we move around in our own space."

Davison hopes that, if anything, this is what has changed in recent years. He concedes that some of the early projects he did in the 1990s were more about showing off your wealth, than creating a comfortable home to live in. "It was all about loft living," he says, "and we were really at the forefront of that. These were factory buildings, they were industrial, and they were part of saying 'I am different'. It was a kind of ego trip, and I think the philosophy of Yoo, and what percolates through in the designs of the studio, is that it doesn't really serve any purpose at the end of the day to make your apartment this kind of celebration of your ego, or your potential as a high earner. Far more important is that home is somewhere you can nurture your family, and be with friends, a place that totally functions around your needs. We can make it look fabulous too, but more important are the bones that lie underneath it."

Storage and utility spaces

With this in mind, Yoo Design Studio insist on storage space when they are planning the layout of an apartment. Working globally, they have found attitudes towards storage vary from country to country. This is mainly because some property developers feel constrained by the fact that it takes away from the square footage of a property, since you can't always measure into wardrobes or cupboard space when you sell. As Davison puts it: "We fight for storage, we think it's essential. If we can't actually build fitted storage, we make sure that there's space to retrofit it. In Russia, for instance, they require huge amounts of storage, even in a one-bedroom place – I guess they have more clothes to wear, and big furry coats." According to Davison, most countries also now demand dedicated utility spaces, even if it's just a cupboard with a dryer stacked on top of a washing machine, or a washing machine and dryer side by side that allows for a clothes rail above them. "That's very much standard now, across the globe," admits Davison, "and so we just always do it." His conclusion is that having some sort of utility space, even in a small one-bedroom apartment, is not just about giving up that extra square metre of space in the living room, "because that makes no difference, but being able to have the ability to hide away your laundry does. Otherwise you have a washing machine grinding away in the corner, with your washing out on display, and there has to be a way of managing that."

ABOVE The City palette is inspired by an urbane cityscape to create white, neutral, reflective interiors that contrast with the neon and glitz outside.

OPPOSITE A predominately white and grey interior is accented with yellow. A 1960s Saarinen chair with turquoise Kenzo corduroy contrasts strikingly with red stools. The kitchen has suspended Lladro lights.

Cutting-edge comfort

Davison attempts to balance a very human need for comfort, with something that's cutting-edge and architecturally exciting in the city. For this reason, the City palette includes dark, black wenge wood floors: "It's just a bit more contemporary and stronger than blond wood, which is too soft in this setting. You want something sharper here," says Davison. As well as being more urban, a black finish gives a clearer dimension to the floor, and can make a room look deeper, providing the optical illusion of a larger space.

Similarly, because the walls throughout are white, keeping the kitchen worktops in white Corian with matt white laminate units avoids too many changes in material. The overall theme should be unifying, seamless and as expansive as possible. Polished stainless steel adds a sharp, clean edge, and it's reflective. "Steel has the ability to make a space look brighter and more open," reveals Julieann Humphryes, who works alongside Davison creating the palettes.

In order to add a more comfortable layer, and avoid the whole interior becoming too harsh, neutral grey rugs are introduced on the floor. These are in keeping with a more monochrome palette, but they also add texture. Grey is simple and understated; the notion of using bolder colours is simply not part of the unadulterated City palette. "You also don't want to add too much pattern as it will make the space look smaller, so stick to solid tones," adds Humphryes. Optional fur throws add extra texture and make the space feel far more luxurious and sexy – a solid white fur throw, for instance, adds texture without being too bold a statement.

Davison's advice is to keep furnishings sleek and simple – mix it up a bit by adding a vintage piece here and there, but in general low coffee tables and the pure, clean lines of a contemporary leather sofa will suit a small space better. Add impact to the City palette with large art pieces that provide an essential art gallery vibe. Whether they are on the wall or are sculptural pieces, they create a cosmopolitan, cultural feel and add a bit of life to the interior. Edge lighting (concealed lighting that runs around the edge of the ceiling or floor) adds to this mood, as do contemporary flooring and table lamps. Starck's gold Gun lamp, for instance, adds a bit of excitement and proves that in a small space lighting can be multifunctional by not just providing light, but also acting as a unique sculptural element in a room.

Yoo Design Studio also aim to avoid designing dedicated office spaces within their apartments. Instead, they are more inclined to set up work areas using furniture. Whenever they include a sofa they always have a narrow table along the back, similar to the traditional French console table, which usually faces into the room. "The console table used to be a purely decorative thing," explains Davison, "but now you can put a great chair behind it and immediately it becomes the little office space, which is so much better than having a desk shoved up against a wall or in a boring room somewhere on its own. We've all got laptops and it's a much more casual approach to work – you're living in your home, not stuck in this study. Some people need that enclosed space, but it's not something we encourage."

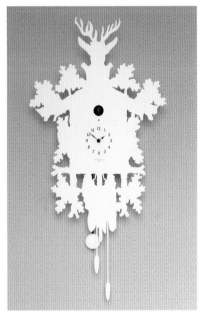

ABOVE A playful take on a Jagdstück "cuckoo" clock, this modern white clock by Pascal Tarabay is shaped like the silhouette of a traditional cuckoo clock, with a deer head and a small, red cuckoo that pops out to announce the hour, but without any of the traditional, three-dimensional woodworking found in more typical clocks. The minimalist design of Tarabay's clock is accentuated by the yellow and grey Art of Wallpaper lining.

LEFT Small city residences benefit from the use of a limited white colour palette to create an illusion of space. Edge lighting avoids any intrusive lamp fixtures, allowing the overall impression to be clean, airy and light.

TOP RIGHT The eaves in this interior are lined with various photographs in silver-leaf frames on one side and mirrors on the opposite side. This has the combined effect of adding interest and drama to the entrance hall.

YOO DESIGN STUDIO

How does Yoo Design Studio work?

We work alongside all of the Yoo designers, often interpreting their ideas so we can synthesize and take what we've learned from them, bringing all of this knowledge together into Yoo studio. There's inbuilt intelligence in the studio, and we're not just hanging on the shirt-tails of Starck or any of the other designers. We've probably got 11 designers in the studio here, some are architects and some are interior designers, but because of the nature of our job, those boundaries have really become blurred.

What is the thinking behind the various palettes?

With the palettes we are trying to create something that is quite specific and clearly defined. It may well be influenced by a particular place or location, but that's just the starting point and the idea is that this then provides a guide, an opportunity for individuals to explore their own style. People love the palettes because they trust that we know how to select a basic set of materials, and it's completely edited down, so it's simple to comprehend. With the City palette, for instance, you have a dark and a light palette, almost day and night, and with Country it's something softer and less hard-edged.

Are your design ideas viable for the average person?

We've honed our craft designing apartments for city dwellers, over many years now, and we're really keen to not be in the elite bracket – we love the idea of good design for many people, and not merely the few. Our theory is that we should definitely be producing good design that doesn't necessarily cost a lot of money: designing an apartment is not just about materials and fancy finishes, it's essentially about how the various spaces function and interact.

Is there a set process for designing an apartment?

Good apartment design is all about how people will eventually use that space. We primarily look at the living space, how we arrive into that space, and the rational arrangement of openings off it, keeping some sort of symmetry and strength. It's not to do with finish or wallpaper or anything like that, it's just, literally, plasterboard walls and how the space within is arranged.

Ideally the second or third bedroom should open up into the main living room, and the kitchen is part of the living space, situated in some way that makes it simple to close off or keep open – it could be sliding walls or a series of openings with storage in them. We always want "fat" walls, so there's that potential for storage. Our interiors are actually quite simple spaces, but they are set up to make sure they are flexible, that the room can be rearranged. It's not that the TV has to go in one place, and the dining table in another, nothing is static or fixed. It's always a space that allows for different arrangements.

What about lighting?

Most of our lighting now is concealed or freestanding, except where we add drama with a chandelier. Lots of fixed, overhead lighting, with spotlights in the ceiling is great for the cleaner, but not for someone living there. Lighting where the whole ceiling is studded with low voltage downlighters or spots – it's too much like a shoe shop. The light it creates is not particularly pleasant, and the fittings mean it's a nightmare to change the bulbs.

If you have a huge penthouse, we think complicated, sophisticated lighting is part of that whole – a penthouse is, by definition, a kind of stage to be on display. However, most people live in fairly cellular, relatively small spaces, and complicated lighting systems in small spaces just make no sense. It's too expensive, it's unnecessary, and you can do so much more with the money. We'd rather have a lamp that's on a stand, with a couple of task lights that you can move around the room. One of the key things we do is put plug sockets in the floor, which allows you to have lamps in the middle of the room. They are all such great designs now, and you can change the mood of a room by repositioning them really easily.

Coloured lighting is all a bit of a gimmick really. It's fun for restaurants and hotel lobbies, people want what they see in these places, but it's something you probably play with for a week. You can't sit in red lighting for more than about half an hour before you start to go a bit crazy with it.

So what is it that makes a home individual and real?

The idea that everything can move around and change is what keeps us all feeling a little bit energized. You almost want some mistakes, and you want stuff that doesn't work sometimes just so you can humanize a place. It's what creates the pearl, it's the piece of sand in the oyster. Without that, you will be dissatisfied or bored and want to change it anyway, so don't get too hung up about it.

In some cases you need that perfectly defined space, you want to walk into an airport and see everything absolutely pristine because you want to be confident that those aeroplanes are going to fly and land technically perfectly, but with a home, well that's different. Striving for the perfect interior at home, you might end up feeling like Patrick Bateman in the business card scene in *American Psycho* – someone will always go that step further and will just highlight your own imperfections, so don't do that to yourself. You want to be comfortable in your own home, so make it a human place to be, and don't be afraid to change it whenever you feel like it. A collection of postcards on the wall, for instance, is something you can rearrange all the time. It's not the Mona Lisa, but what's great is that it's something you can continually change. That's why we love chalkboard walls, anything that is a bit messy, a bit fun, easily transformed.

What would you avoid using in an interior?

Glass blocks are generally a bit recherché – if you look at the Maison de Verre in Paris, they are beautiful when used in a 1930s setting, but they became over-stylized in the early 1990s. They're not awful, it's just that nobody has come up with something original recently.

Also, we'd probably avoid a lot of galvanized steel and metal steps. Our staircases are always hidden or concealed, we never make a big song and dance about them. It's the absolute polar opposite of where we were in the 1990s – especially after Eva Jiricna did a glass one for the Joseph store on Sloane Street in London – where you would try to make a feature of a staircase. In a home, as opposed to a shop, you have to spend a disproportionate amount of money to make a stair look really brilliant and sculptural, otherwise it can look a little bit clumpy. We'd rather spend the money elsewhere, and I would prefer one amazing light fitting in a double-height space, than end up with an exulted "show" staircase.

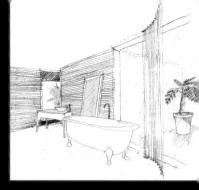

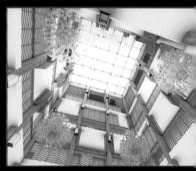

TOP An early sketch for Yoo Phuket, by Julieann Humphryes. The bath is positioned to enjoy a view of the private garden. The floor-mounted taps give a luxurious feel to the simple room.

CENTRE David Archer's first sketch for the lobby of Downtown by Starck. The chandelier, the largest of its day, was originally made for JP Morgan.

ABOVE An early sketch for the Adam building in Split, by Julieann Humphryes, David Archer and Flick, shows a quadruple-height space with a glass lantern roof and four chandeliers.

URBAN.

classic
timeless elegance
luxury
east meets west
eclectic design
couture
home from home
texture
clean lines
symmetry

KELLY HOPPEN for **yoo**

URBAN

The linear, muted tones and use of repeated motifs in this scheme are familiar to anyone who has followed Hoppen's work. "This is very much the Kelly Hoppen brand look," says Hoppen, "It's lots of straight lines and timeless elegant luxury." This look is the distillation of many years of Hoppen refining her signature style. "I see this scheme relating to a permanent home rather than a weekend or holiday place," says Hoppen. "It has my usual mix of sumptuous fabric, such as linen and crushed and plain velvet chenille, in my tight neutral colour palette." Flashes of burnt orange and red, however, also make an appearance. "I think that an ideal background is a pleasing neutral that allows you to place items within that react with it. The red and orange create a lift, and can bring out different traits in the other fabrics." Hoppen believes this allows a home to keep evolving and to be able to withstand the addition and subtraction of various pieces, as taste and lifestyle develop. "This is the look most people know me for, and it has worked time and time again for many people. It is very good at accommodating individual style because it represents a way of life, not just a look. It's something that people can live in, responding to their every need, but they can also imprint their own identity too; I always believe a home isn't a home until you have all your special bits in it."

The horn buttons on cushions and dark wood mixed with stone are all hallmarks of Hoppen's approach to creating sensuous urban spaces. But as well as using these iconic elements, she has latterly experimented with form, deviating from her trademark angular look. "I've become more interested in feminine shapes, and as I worked on my last home it felt softer as a result. I have moved away from purely straight lines, and I think the combination of the curved and sequential lines has created a real sense of balance." Hoppen has reflected this in her choice of furniture. "I love my Modenature six white leather chairs surrounding my wenge table. It's very sculptural. They represent this idea very well."

Hoppen is also known for homes with the "wow" factor, whether that is through enhancing or creating an architectural detail, such as a double-height room or padded doors, but she insists that this can also be achieved on a more modest level. "If a home does not have any existing features to suggest drama, a lot can be done to create it. Try a unique 'star piece' of furniture", suggests Hoppen, "such as an incredibly large vase, or a piece of challenging art, even a Perspex piano. Any of those will demand serious attention."

Outdoor entertainment spaces

Often city homes have limited outdoor spaces, but even a small garden, balcony or roof terrace can provide a respite from the busy pace of modern living and be used to extend your living and entertaining areas. "There is no such thing as designing for outdoor entertaining," says Hoppen. "There is simply entertaining. Essentially

ABOVE The Urban palette is consistently neutral, comprising off-whites, creams and taupe for paints and textiles, grounded by dark stained-wood finishes to create a balanced and harmonious approach. Contrasting textures within the limited theme provide visual interest.

OPPOSITE The muted hues of this outdoor scheme allow it to nestle into, rather than compete with, the rooftop cityscape. Accessories are understated: floor-standing lanterns for night-time lighting and container plants that facilitate a reconfiguration of the space according to occasion or mood.

you need to start with the same considerations: budget, space allocation, and aesthetic, and then you need to consider how the space will be used. The way that people interact in a space is all to do with how well you have set the scene." When planning the space, the advantages offered by the locale should first be considered. "Do you want to look at the skyline, a bank of trees? Essentially you can create your focal point, or more than one if you are zoning the area for different purposes, wherever you like." The arrangement of lounging sofas around a large, low-level table for example, can create a sense of intimacy even under a vast sky, especially with the addition of candlelight. "It is essential that any terrace or garden is seen as an extension of the house's interior design to ensure that there is harmony, and must always be planned in conjunction, from the beginning," states Hoppen. "The best garden rooms are an extension of the aesthetic ambitions of the house."

Practical concerns do, however, vary when considering the challenges of an outdoor room. "Of course, materials need to be hardy," says Hoppen. "There are literally thousands of waterproof fabrics available now, so there is no need to compromise on the look you want. The kind of fabrics we use can withstand a heavy shower, but of course need to be stored over winter. But something like wood can be chosen specifically because it will age, possibly become silvered as time passes. You can plan for how the piece will develop over time when you select it. One of my favourite pieces was an old Indian table that I used on a roof terrace and it became such a wonderful feature."

The less exciting issues of plumbing and electrical details must be considered before the enjoyable job of choosing the decorative aspects. Successful irrigation and appropriate lighting will determine the lasting success of your outdoor space. It is also important to investigate any natural potential. "Where does the sun fall and at what time of day? Is that the spot to consider a dining area for long summer lunches? And if this is a space you want to enjoy year round, evergreens are preferable; they can give you greenery throughout the year and can be teased into very pleasing, symmetrical forms. The same is true of a water feature. The play of light and shadow can offer constant interest."

The size of the space also heavily influences the treatment. A large roof terrace may need careful zoning with the demarcation of clear boundaries, dividing the purpose and atmosphere of various places, by using furniture and lighting, rather than walls. "It is important not to leave the mood to chance," says Hoppen, "even if you think you have less control because you are out in the elements. You can easily transform a space that is happily comfortable for sunbathing and brunch into a glamorous night-time party scene. Recessed floor-level lighting, a fire pit or even some kind of elegant awning can extend the night-time appeal of your outside space." But ultimately, Hoppen's personal cocktail for good entertaining takes more than a glorious location. "Of course, you can create the most stunning environment, but that alone will not create an incredible party. The two elements you really have to get right on the night are music and people."

TOP Splashes of burnt orange are enhanced by the vivid green plants in a stained-wood corridor, while the rounded plant containers break up the angular bench seating arrangement.

ABOVE Aesthetics are considered from every angle; a low-level circular wenge table surrounded by white Modénature Plaza bridge chairs creates a pleasing sculptural form when not in use.

OVERLEAF LEFT Bathing is elevated to the level of meditation with the serene repetition of curvaceous and linear forms, enhanced by the gold cube cut-out table and white stool.

OVERLEAF RIGHT Pared-back but also practical, this dressing room fulfils the wish list of every wardrobe mistress. Arranging clothing and shoes by tonal colours gives consistency and organization to the room.

OPPOSITE A 1960s Eero Aarnio bubble chair is a clever device to enhance the double height of this London loft space, converted from a Victorian schoolroom. In the background, Kelly's black ring screen emphasizes the geometrical elements.

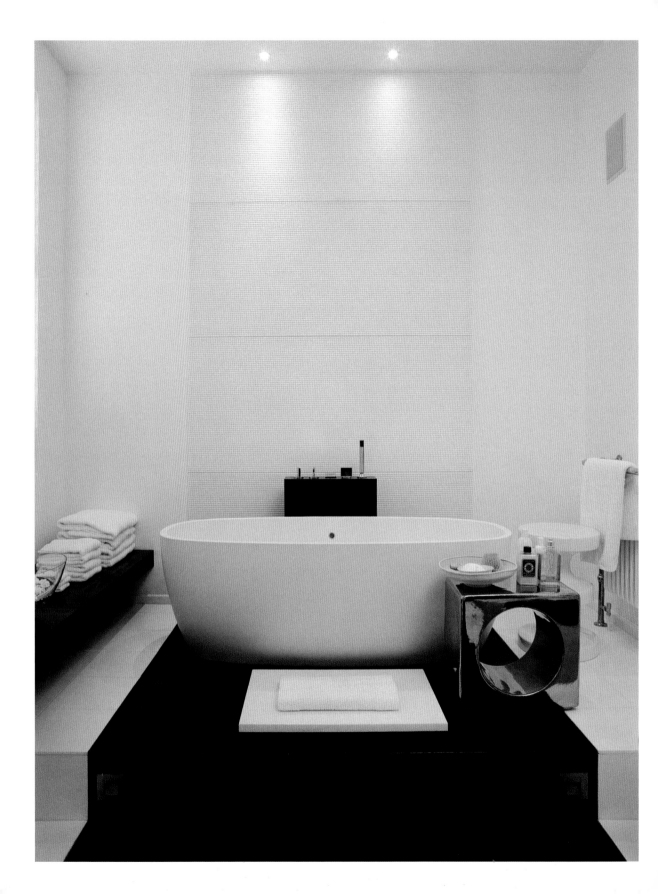

DISCO.

geometrics
shine
mirror
mosaic
plush
crystal
mercedes coupé
sheepskin
david bowie
orchids
'70s halston

JADE JAGGER for **yoo**

DISCO

Most people's childhood homes don't recall the glamour of Studio 54, Halston and the glittering New York 1970s disco scene. But for Jade Jagger, child of two of the era's icons (Bianca and Mick), the sumptuous *louche décor* of the era represents the comfort of home. "It's a very personal scheme, and when we considered who would live here, we imagined a woman who is very social, comfortable in her own skin and bold. A bit like me!," explains Jagger. "For me, it's a very feminine scheme and in some ways reflects my jewellery design with the shiny surfaces and burnished gold."

The scheme manages to combine classical sumptuousness and urban edge. Some of the design details, such as the shag pile carpets, velvet, tinted mirror and suede are very much true to the period, and work so well mainly due to the confident way in which they are applied. "We weren't limited by a common sense of aesthetics," says Jade's business partner, Tom Bartlett. "Nor were we afraid of the suggestion of slightly bad taste." As a result, the scheme invokes the best of the era. The pair chose for example, the Tulip table by Eero Saarinen, produced by the Knoll furniture company in 1956, in one of its original incarnations in a bold, white marble. It sits alongside napa suede-covered furniture, which seems at once modern and referential to the heydays of these materials. Jagger elaborates, "It's very important to have a combination of icons that aren't just about good taste. It conjures up that era; when I see sheepskin I just sense that warmth and indulgence. It breaks up that modernist austerity."

"We see this as a hanging-out, comfortable space," says Bartlett, "and found ourselves looking at photographs of people sitting in a conversation pit, fabulously dressed and holding a cocktail glass with an olive." The pair came up with a more practical solution to the idea of spontaneous entertaining than a dedicated conversation pit. The Pod, exclusive to the Jade condominiums in New York City, is a freestanding unit containing the kitchen appliances and wardrobe space and available in a black, white or gold finish. It can be closed up to instantly turn an informal living space into the perfect backdrop for a party, while serving the dual purpose of providing a room divider. This ability to entertain at will is very much in keeping with the spirit of glitzy Studio 54 hedonism.

Reflective surfaces and shiny pop culture references

Central to the palette are hues of gold, silver, pearl, white and sand. The idea of precious materials and indulgence are reinforced by the use of shimmering and reflective surface. "Mirror is a great way to create an illusion of depth and space. It's also amazingly neutral," explains Jagger. "It can help a room in many ways, such as by balancing an open elevation with a matching mirrored panel. It is useful for drawing the eye and creating a focal point, especially in more subdued tinted or semi-reflective finishes. It looks amazing around fireplaces, for example." The pair even go as far as devoting whole rooms to mirrored surfaces. Bartlett elaborates,

ABOVE The Disco palette comprises natural woods, white and taupe set against glittering touches such as disco balls, crystals and mirrored surfaces. An shot of bright colour in yellow , orange or pink lifts the theme to create an eye-popping and energetic vibe.

OPPOSITE TOP In this Jade condominium apartment in New York City, the gold lacquered central Pod structure contains all the practical wardrobe and kitchen hardware in an open-plan space, and works as a divider to separate bedroom and living areas. A series of Warhol-style celebrity paintings inject colour on the far wall.

OPPOSITE Corian white keeps kitchen surfaces open and light on the reverse side of the Pod. The use of a large Rêves du Désert rug defines the boundary between dining and lounge areas, and picks up the bright orange and pink used as accents throughout, while a reflective coffee table bounces colour from the floor. Johnny B Good lights by Ingo Maurer appear over the dining table.

"We often fill entire spaces with mirrored mosaics to break down the edges of a small space. But it's always worth considering what will be reflected back at you when planning these things – perhaps mirroring the back of a loo door isn't such a great idea."

Light, whether natural or electric, also gets the mirror treatment. Natural light is maximized by artful placing of surfaces to bounce it back into the room, turning a potentially plain wall into an illusory window, and Bartlett is keen to invert the idea of the staid ceiling fixture. "A mirror ball always works instead of the expected chandeliers," he comments, "and adds a sense that someone might start dancing at any moment, which is always good." This ability to party wherever and whenever within a space is reinforced by Jagger. "The idea of the feel of an open-plan warehouse felt really right to me," says Jagger. "There's something of Warhol's Factory about it."

The shiny aspects of pop culture also feature heavily, with recognizable design classics positioned alongside the "of the moment" design cover-style imagery in picture frames. The images create an instant connection with the viewer, calling upon our collective cultural memory, and invoking inevitable associations. For some, this would be purely iconographic, but Jagger's own experience has a more personal strand to it – she knew Andy Warhol and, it is fair to say, he had an impact on her style. "It's true, I did grow up in the midst of all that 1970s glamour, hanging out with my parent's friends, and Warhol was part of that," acknowledges Jagger. "I knew him from being a small child, and I hung out at the Factory; you could say I was slightly schooled there. I did some things on paintings using diamond dust, stuff like that."

One of the two farthest reaching effects on her was her belief in collaboration. "The Factory was a real team and the experience was shared," remembers Jagger. One of the team's now-iconic favourites, the disco ball, "is something we have become known for," laughs Jagger. "Playfulness is a big part of pop art. It really embraces bold colour and always projects a sense of youthfulness. I also love the fact that it is populist and was rooted in the everyday." With such common interests, it is not surprising that Warhol was quoted as saying "My favourite Jagger is Jade".

Rather than revering the pop culture it presents, Bartlett suggests that their use "can take the pomp out of an interior set-piece, make it more approachable". The items chosen, however, should reflect the personal, rather than the publicly approved. "Use things that mean something to you," says Jagger, "not some randomly trendy items. Groups of things that are inherently pop or even kitsch gives these things a collective meaning, but one randomly placed figurine of a puppy might be taken entirely at face value." Bartlett finishes: "There is a careful line to tread here between funny and personal and arch and cynical."

Mirror is a great way to add an illusion of depth and space. It's also amazingly neutral. It is useful for drawing the eye and creating a focal point, especially in more subdued tinted or semi-reflective finishes.

TOP A series of Mirror Ball lights by Tom Dixon hang in a mirrored mosaic-lined entrance for the ultimate Disco look.

ABOVE Custom-made Moroccan lattice-worked windows throw patterns of light into a living area.

OPPOSITE Outdoor terrace furniture by Gandia Blasco, including day beds and bench seating, provides perfect lounging for day or evening.

JADE JAGGER

TOM BARTLETT

How did you get here?

JADE: We met 15 years ago when Tom decorated a flat for my then boyfriend. I got involved in the process and we really enjoyed working together, so we kept doing it. Since then we have collaborated on many projects such as my house in Ibiza and the shop interiors for Garrard.
TOM: Jade knew John socially and he had admired her home in Ibiza and her jewellery design. He thought that her style could translate very well to the Yoo concept.

What do you both bring to the collaboration?

TOM: I trained as an architect so had a very design-education based process. I'd tried very hard to be a modernist but failed miserably because although I like clean lines and a well functioning space, I prefer it set against something old or decorative. Jade's approach was very different, or so I thought. Designing jewellery is not about function, it has no practical use, it's highly decorative and talismanic. But watching Jade work I realized that there is an evolved story behind every collection she creates.
JADE: Tom's technical grounding was at first a sort of touchstone for me to understand what was possible, such as learning how to set up a grid system or how to build certain structures. But now we're both involved in all aspects; Tom is as likely to come up with a decorative detail as I am an architectural concept.

How does working for Yoo fit into this?

TOM: The Yoo concept is about creating bespoke environments for the individual, giving them some tools to develop their own sense of style and creativity. We meet developers and talk about what they need. Then we get together in the studio and make plans, sorting through the priorities before we start playing creatively.

How do you begin your process?

JADE: I like to think very logically about how a space will be used. It really needs to flow well and suit its purpose. Once we have the practical base working we think about a furniture plan. We purposely keep the flooring and walls quite neutral so we can apply strong decorative touches.

When putting your mood boards and palettes together, where do you find ideas and inspiration?

TOM: I think Jade and I design with a client in mind, or a corporation. For Yoo we create an imaginary person that embodies each of the four schemes. Considering who might live there, and how, gives us a depth of understanding and as a result we create a better scheme. And then we talk about the practical issues, such as the specific parameters created by each property.
JADE: For example, on the Jade, the New York West 19th Street project, we were dealing with open-concept living spaces and we wanted to maximize the flexibility by using the Pod concept, a freestanding unit containing the kitchen and storage elements. But we still wanted it to feel luxurious; we tried to create the feeling of being in a jewellery box.

What is your dream future project?

JADE: We have always wanted to design a development in India. We are both fascinated by it and think it would be incredibly inspiring. Possibly a rural setting, something where we can create a master plan.
TOM: Tokyo would be our other favourite. In Tokyo it would be really exciting to design tiny, beautifully appointed apartments, highly detailed and stylized.

What strategies can you recommend to those beginning a project?

TOM: A beautiful room always helps but it's really all about maximizing the best of what you have. Things don't have to be perfect. If there is a bit of broken cornice, leave it, it's part of the buildings history.

JADE: A few strong architectural statements are essential. At Garrard we created a sterling silver wall. Or the mirror mosaic hallway in our disco scheme is truly arresting.

TOM: And pace the spaces with a different rhythm, so that they have different moods. But also a unifying element can be very effective. In a project in Turkey, we used a ribbon of tiles on the kitchen work surface that turns into a table then runs all the way outside. It linked the whole space together.

What is the key to a really exceptional, rather than simply a pleasant space?

TOM: You must have things that have meaning, that's what makes the strongest statement, irrespective of what they look like. Personal history is very important. So if you have granny's chair, a bit ugly but a loving reminder, you can still always make it work. It's what really makes a home.

JADE: Collections, groupings of objects or themes really work. Is also interesting to subvert objects. Change a piece or reinterpret it with an unexpected fabric or finish. That way you avoid safeness. It's important to take risks.

JADE AND TOM'S 10 STYLE RULES TO BREAK

1 "Never paint a small room black." Paint it whatever colour you like.

2 "Your bathroom should never be bigger than your bedroom." We love big bathrooms. You spend most of your "me" time in there so it shouldn't be resigned to a cramped space.

3 "Cutting-edge design is essential." Looking at classic design is a great starting point; we love the Parisian Chanel apartment, historic fabrics, Porto Santos Stefano.

4 "Throw out your crap." We like things you collect along the way – just recreate them and see what you think.

5 "You can make any space fantastic." Well-planned space is the key.

6 "Wait and save up for good art." Shove a good magazine cover in a frame until you can find and afford what you like.

7 "Neutral is beige." Neutral is gold, silver, black, white, and pink (if you live in India).

8 "Fluorescence is for highlighting markers and road worker jackets." Fluorescent spray paint is an essential decorating tool.

9 "Get a great sofa in front of your TV." Make a bed niche in your TV room for the ultimate recline.

10 "Harmony is in carefully matching your objects." Harmony is in expressing yourself through enjoying your interiors.

TOP Jagger and Bartlett create their schemes for a thoughtfully considered imaginary client. This bedroom plan, drawn by Tom Bartlett, includes a fireplace; a prominent feature in many Jade Jagger interiors.

ABOVE Jagger uses the butterfly motif throughout many of her interiors; they almost always appear in groupings, where they have a collective impact, rather than as singular images.

NATURE.

raw leather
stone
wood
linen
cotton
beech
beach
alvar aalto
alps
fjords
fur trees
leaf
bark
weathered paint

yoo inspired by STARCK

NATURE

"Our Nature palette is for those people who love to live with fresh air, blue sky, the smell of the rising sun, purity, simplicity," describes Philippe Starck. This palette draws its inspiration from the widespread and deep-rooted desire of city dwellers to bring nature into the urban environment. Most obviously this takes the form of window boxes, vases of flowers and the creation of parks and gardens. But most of us also collect small objects as reminders of a beautiful walk or a sunny day at the seaside… we love to keep pebbles and seashells on our desk or windowsill, and might treasure a piece of silver-grey driftwood, a handful of pine cones or a colourful feather.

Our instinctive longing to remain connected to nature, even in the most sophisticated and built-up places, has been pursued since the earliest people began to settle. "We need to remember where we came from," says Starck. In his own life, Starck makes frequent forays into nature when he stays at his various cabins around the world. Of course he is always working and sketching, but here, through the largest possible windows, he likes to absorb views of the landscape, watch the birds and get in touch with simplicity. "Nature is a young woman running on the beach, the day is new and full of fresh perfume," he describes. "We could be in Sweden and there will be pale wood, natural linen, everything is green and light and fresh."

The colours and materials of the Nature palette are drawn from a gentle spectrum of natural hues – pale, sun- and sea-bleached wood, and sand and pebble-grey mixed with a soft green. However, Starck believes that in selecting a style for decorating a room, we should take care to explore our responses to different elements of interior design. The most successful interiors can be created when clients are in touch with their inner feelings and understand why they make their selections. "When it comes to interior design, I am not interested in whether yellow looks good with white, or whether cubes are good with rectangles. I want to know what all of this means. How will these colours and materials and shapes have an impact on your life."

He encourages clients to make their own decisions and believes that the palettes provide a shortcut to finding a style that you can live with. "If you employ an interior designer, there is a danger that you will end up living in someone else's brain. The designer will make a place that shows off his or her talents so they can make the front page of a design magazine. This is terrible. With the palettes we know that people will be better equipped at making their own home in the way that they like."

Bringing the countryside into the town

In using this Nature palette, Starck brings his own interpretation of *rus in urbe* (the Latin phrase meaning "countryside in the town"). For him, Nature is not about

ABOVE Referring to themes found in the natural world, the Nature palette incorporates Arabescato marble, white oiled oak and colours in pale green, white and taupe.

OPPOSITE Gentle natural hues tie together a diverse range of furniture and accessories – an Argentinian cowhide rug, a rose-print upholstered chair and a Muletas floorstanding light by Dalí.

The artist is
in the men's
room.
He will be right
back.

Tell me
a story
so I won't
feel asleep.

borrowing organic forms; instead the elements of his palette can be deployed in literal and symbolic ways. The literal theme uses unadorned items that are drawn directly from nature – a cowhide rug, a vase of the most delicious white lilies, a decorative bowl of fruit, or fine slabs of marble. More symbolically, nature can appear one step removed from its original state as, for example, a highly graphic image of trees on wallpaper, a standard lamp with a curious, bone-inspired stem, or in a silver-painted chair with arms in the form of folded bird wings.

When it comes to objects in the room, Starck says we should think and choose carefully. "Not only is it necessary to design within certain moral and ecological parameters, but also we can make objects that can really help us progress as a civilization. Objects can be used to criticise society, to provoke debate. For me, the real success of a design is when it starts a conversation between two people."

Starck clearly has an affinity with the great Scandinavian designers of the twentieth century, and has a great respect for Arne Jacobsen who produced an amazing sequence of design classics from the sculptural Egg chair to the elegant plywood Series 7 chair on metal legs. He also ranks the nature-inspired Finn Alvar Aalto among his roll call of greats. In common with many Scandinavian designers, who understand that light is a precious gift and has a premium, Starck is also a master at handling this ethereal commodity. Crystal chandeliers add an instant sense of luxury, but also reflect and refract light rays around a room in a magical way. Candles might be rather cliché, but they are guaranteed to be romantic, so who could refuse candelabra? He uses white and reflective materials, such as marble and stone, to keep the luxurious and precious light rays moving around the room.

As you would certainly expect with Starck the combinations of objects, furnishings and finishes are always playful. Who else would enjoy a placing a fine, gold-painted Louis XV chair with its detailed floral fabric upholstery on a rustic cowhide rug? Here, the ultimate in sophistication, delicacy and refinement is juxtaposed with a raw and unadorned animal skin.

We are such sophisticated beasts ourselves that we hardly stop to question such a mix, but when we do it is almost shocking. And then there is the near-abstract wallpaper with its tree trunks running between the floor and the ceiling. In traditional buildings these great lengths of wood would form columns to hold up the roof, but these days they are reduced to mere motifs. Nevertheless, it is still fascinating that people choose to line their rooms with symbolic tree images, as if we are in a clearing in the forest. What could be closer to nature than collecting apples and placing them in a bowl at the centre of the table? And how many of us bring flowers into the bathroom? But why not? When we are naked and bathing, we are closest to nature.

…I am not interested in whether yellow looks good with white, or whether cubes are good with rectangles. I want to know what all of this means. How will these colours and materials and shapes have an impact on your life.

TOP Accents of bright colour bring relief to a muted easy-to-live-in palette.

ABOVE The Favela chair by the Campana brothers appears to be constructed of timber offcuts but it is a carefully executed piece. Combined with Cole & Son's Woods wallpaper, it creates an outdoor feel.

OPPOSITE The ceiling light is Cicatrice de Luxe by Starck; the hand-cut crystal vases on a mount have a feel of a bygone age yet merged with modern technology. Cherner walnut and merbau wood-strip flooring, and a Jean Prouvé table and chairs, are complemented by blackboard-painted walls.

ABOVE This Rilievo marble table by Up + Up is cast as a typical pine table but in a luxury material. Two green winged chairs by Belloni and Boffi bring natural bird forms into the interior.

ABOVE The Woods wallpaper from Cole & Son and
a Piero Fornasetti lamp give the impression of light
and shade, sun and shadow.

ABOVE Elongated Venetian-style glass mirrors are hung against a bright yellow wall in an otherwise all-white interior, with variegated pattern supplied by the Arabescato marble floor.

OPPOSITE Balance and symmetry are evident in a white Thassos tiled bathroom at the Gramercy, New York. Neat lines and geometrics are given relief with circular themes, as in the devil's eye wood stool by Pols Potter.

OVERLEAF The grey veining of the marble in this all-Arabescato bathroom is the only adornment necessary to create a dramatic showpiece.

NATURAL.

cosy
soft
pillows
homey
warm
balance
off-white

WANDERS & *yoo*

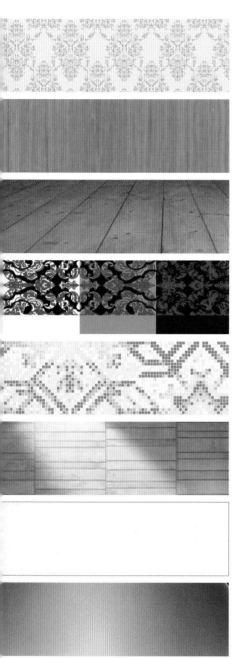

NATURAL

With the Natural palette, Marcel Wanders creates interior spaces that are all about invoking a sense of warmth and comfort. As the name suggests, the palette employs natural materials, natural forms and natural colours. Wanders says that Natural is related to the Architectural palette, but whereas that palette celebrates the urban and the minimal, Natural aims to soften the hard edge of city properties. "This palette is connected to the Architectural palette, but in a kind of sensuous way, a kind of warm way," explains Wanders. "It's a more warm area. We use, as the name suggests, more natural materials. We use natural colours. It isn't too loud, although some people will feel it is still pretty strong! Our design often has a very urban and hard expression, so I think there could be the need for a language that is not so hard, a little bit less urban."

Breaking down artificiality

The keywords associated with the Natural palette hint at the feelings of sensuous comfort it seeks to give off: cosy, soft, pillows, homey, warm, balance, off-white. "We give people the opportunity to have a kind of natural surrounding around them," Wanders continues. "We live in concrete houses, and our bodies cannot live in concrete houses; architecture can be too artificial and too hard. So this is the concept that tries to create the least artificial surrounding of all the palettes." One way that Wanders hopes to achieve this sense of softness and sensuality is through the use of rounded, organic forms instead of hard-edged ones. Irregular, free form and harmonious, organic shapes are very easy to live with, as they visually recall the natural world.

Wanders has produced many furniture and product designs that employ pebble-like shapes. His coffee tables for Italian mosaic brand Bisazza are natural-looking rock shapes that are decorated with colourful, floral motifs; and his Soapstars range of baths and basins, also for Bisazza, resemble rounded, scooped-out bars of soap. Wanders' Zen range of furniture for Dutch brand Moooi also uses organic forms; the range featured an object called Zen Stone – a rounded, hollow form on legs – that could be used as a freestanding storage device.

Another way to break down artificiality is through the use of natural, or at least natural-looking, materials and nonindustrial processes. Again Wanders has designed several products in this vein. His seminal Knotted chair – the design that sealed his reputation on the international stage – is made of hand-knotted rope and described as "a marriage of handicraft and industrial technology"; as part of Dry Tech project, the soft, pliable fibres that construct the chair are made strong, rigid and durable. Known for using natural materials in unexpected ways, Wanders also employed a natural sponge as a mould for his porcelain Sponge vase.

ABOVE The warm tones of the Natural palette are achieved through the use of oak and plank flooring, and taupe, white and gold wallpapers and white matt paint. Carpets in rich warm colours add cosiness, while taupe and white mosaics and Mosa tiles are used in the bathrooms.

OPPOSITE A head board of a moon adds a luminous touch to a bedroom that has dramatic views to the outdoors, and creates a feeling of natural serenity.

Materials specified for the palette include oak plank flooring in living areas, and Mosa tiles and Bisazza mosaics in the bathrooms. Wanders has created various glass tile projects for Bisazza, including furniture and accessories in addition to wall tiles. The Natural palette also includes Suzanne and Stella wallpaper designs from Wanders' Couture range for Graham & Brown. The Suzanne pattern, one of the two specified for Natural interiors, is a black and grey damask featuring metallic and gloss finishes and inlaid with a pattern fill detail. Stella, the other pattern specified, features a gold honeycomb layout with a regal inset motif.

The Couture wallpaper range, launched in 2008, has a similar philosophy behind it to the Natural palette: to soften architectural space and make it more inhabitable for the human body. "I love the hard definition of architectural space," Wanders says of the wallpaper range. "I love the naked fragility of the human body. Unfortunately the naked human body cannot live in clean architectural space. We need interiors because architecture is too technically hard and rational to live in. Therefore I love to blur the boundaries between architecture and interior, between walls and furniture, between furniture and fashion. As our fashion dresses our bodies, wallpaper dresses our walls. Wallpaper and fashion mediate between our naked bodies and architecture. In this way, architecture and man can live together with the sophisticated illusion of Couture."

The lighting used in Natural interiors is, logically, gentler than the other palettes. "In the Natural one, of course, I think the light is a bit softer, the shadows less hard," says Wanders.

. . . I love to blur the boundaries between walls and furniture, between furniture and fashion. Our fashion dresses our bodies, wallpaper dresses our walls.

OPPOSITE TOP The most natural form of all in an interior setting: calla lilies in a vase are displayed against a floral wallpaper. This Delft Blue vase by Marcel Wanders reinterprets a traditional ceramic piece from the Dutch Royal Delft for Moooi.

OPPOSITE The Zen coffee table and Zen stone were inspired by the perfect order and tranquility of a Japanese garden. The hollow, rounded organic form can be used as storage.

OVERLEAF LEFT A wetroom in the Lute Suites, Amsterdam, is decorated with Bisazza Snowflake mosaic tiles and minimalist Gobi basin and fixtures from Boffi. A quiet taupe-toned interior keeps the Natural palette relaxed and subdued.

OVERLEAF RIGHT With its organic bulbous shape, the freestanding Soapstars bath is the centrepiece of the bathroom. Plank flooring and exposed ceiling beams complete the Natural look.

TOP AND ABOVE The use of colour, pattern and organic material, like Moooi's Smoke Chair and the hand-cast ceramic Haiku plate for B&B Italia, give a natural feeling to the spaces.

COUNTRY.

breeze
bicycle
cut grass
storm lanterns
earth
weathered
cotton
reclaimed
lemonade
sisal
lavender
enamel
aga
seasonal

yoo design studio

COUNTRY

For a design studio based in London, creating a Country palette was not necessarily an obvious or natural progression, but Yoo Design Studio has managed to transform what might otherwise have been a tired, repetitive and well-worn idiom into something fresh and meaningful. "What we are trying to create here is not so much a twee interpretation of the countryside, all floral and paint effects, but something that pulls in the essence of nature," explains Mark Davison. "It's much softer, and less hard-edged than what we might do in an urban setting, but we still want to maintain some of that wit, originality and clean modern lines, without being too slick." "There is an element here that is undeniably relaxed," adds Juliann Humphryes, "the whole point about spending time in the country is that the materials you surround yourself with should be able to weather muddy boots, dogs and kids. Sticking to a palette of hard-wearing, natural materials achieves this perfectly."

Light, natural and matt finishes

Country palette paints tend towards natural colours and warm tones – sage green and light aubergine in particular. More obvious earthy tones are carefully sidestepped, and synthetic shades completely shunned. "The greens and pinks we use are hues you might see in an English country garden, leaf greens and the tops of lavender," explains Humphryes. "If we do use pattern, it's definitely not chintz, but evokes the colours and textures of flowers without resorting to more traditional floral patterns." Rather than brilliant white, which would be too stark, work surfaces are kept to an off-white, matt laminate. Other matt finishes are also used, as opposed to anything reflective or glossy that would be too urban and slick. "Satin nickel is ideal for the Country palette," reveals Humphryes, "as you don't want a shiny, polished effect, but a more tender and soft finish." Lighting is also kept simple and is confined to enamel pendant lamps that hang from the ceiling. Harsh downlighters are avoided in favour of softer light from table lamps. There's no place for anything too glamorous or overwhelming in this sort of space. The big dining tables and larger pieces of furniture may well be classic English farmhouse stuff, but they are painted white or stained a light tone. "We avoid anything too heavy, or traditionally brown," confirms Humphryes, "and lighter-looking, old linen upholstery introduces a vintage element."

Although contemporary in approach and outlook, Yoo Design Studio steer away from the latest, most fashionable materials. "We certainly go to the furniture fairs and if we see something that we think is great then we will use it," says Davison, "but in general we are always looking for things we know will have real quality and longevity to them, a timelessness. That's why we love white Carrara marble, it never dates." The studio's approach to using white marble is what really makes it work: "If we use marble in a bathroom, for instance, it's not just behind the loo and the basins – we use it on every surface possible. If you do it with a vengeance, marble takes on a life of its own and

ABOVE The Country palette consists of natural, matt colours and materials, including Portland stone or limestone, Normandy pale oak and sisal for flooring, and satin nickel for hardware and fixtures. Muted warm tones paired with white create an overall light feel, a world away from the traditional English country style. Colours are inspired by nature – plum, sage green and mandarin sorbet.

OPPOSITE Nature and contemporary design work together with a colour palette that is inspired by the evening sunset. Full-height windows and extended outdoor decking create a feeling of seamlessness between the interior and exterior of the building, while the outside lighting is restricted to a gentle, ambient glow which won't disturb any wildlife that might be close by.

rather than being traditional becomes something that is refreshing once again," reveals Davison. One rule of thumb for tiling is to avoid the traditional foot-by-foot size of tile. According to Davison, 400 x 400mm (15.75 x 15.75in) is the perfect dimension for tiling around basins and toilets, which are generally around 400mm (15.75in) wide, as well as showers, normally 800mm (31.5in) wide (exactly two tiles). "It's not something we insist on," concedes Davison, "but it just feels more sane and organized. It's a calming feeling, I think, if you see everything really well laid out with no bad junctions."

Natural oak wood floors are part of the Country palette; oak provides a neutral tone, without being too rustic. A natural finish is essential so the oak is treated according to the studio's specifications to make it hard-wearing, but not too polished. Limestone is also a natural material with a soft, warm tone that marries well with natural oak to create a soft and warm surface. Each individual palette is constructed to help decide which type of flooring best suits the space but there are no hard and fast rules between opting for blond or dark wood, oak or wenge. "Even so," cautions Davison, "if you have a lot of blond wood furniture and you put a dark wood floor down, it is going to look a bit odd, and my advice is that it's also best with floor surfaces to keep it plain – no inset pebbles or swirly motifs. Sometimes people imagine this adds to the excitement of a space, but when we see this happening, we just go in there and paint all the floorboards white."

But as Davison is quick to point out, choosing the right floor to use throughout the space is extremely important. Wherever possible, he suggests always pushing for the best quality material you can afford. "The thin 5mm laminates have that slightly tappy sound to them, and are fine for a utility room," explains Davison, "but not for your main living space." Wider planks are preferable, but they can become disproportionately expensive so it is better to have the same good-quality, narrow planked floor throughout, than to have wider planks in just one area. "Ideally the only place we chop and change flooring is when you hit the bathrooms," says Davison. "With bedrooms the flooring might change because some people want a softer finish like carpet or sisal. This means you might need a simple fine metal edge, but in the bathroom it's pretty straightforward and the stone butts directly up to the timber."

Details like door handles are also important. The studio is adamant about the importance of all of the elements that are regularly felt and touched in the home. "We try to do bigger, taller doors and we love doors that go up to the ceiling," explains Davison, "but if you've only got a standard door, at least put the door handle low, so the proportions work." Yoo Design Studio only ever put door handles at 900mm (35.4in) high and never higher, even on a tall door. Davison explains this logic by pointing out that if you go into a 1960s house, often everything is at eye level, including door handles and light switches. "Now a lot of people might argue this kind of makes sense, because that is the level that's in our sight line," says Davison. "We don't. Even if it's a boringly proportioned room, if you set everything [light switches and door handles] at 900mm (35.4in) it makes a huge difference to those proportions, and the ceilings will automatically feel higher."

ABOVE Bringing natural objects, such as rough-hewn wood, indoors extends the connection with the outside world. The custom-made planter on the deck also takes the interior experience outside to a view that overlooks the lake.

OPPOSITE The simplicity of tongue-and-groove kitchen units, balanced by an extra-deep white Corian worktop, achieves a calming balance. The twig chairs were made to order from Christian Liaigre. The lamps above the dining table are from Gervasoni.

The whole point about spending time in the country is that the materials you surround yourself with should be able to weather muddy boots, dogs and kids… sticking to a palette of hard-wearing, natural materials achieves this perfectly.

SEA BREEZES.

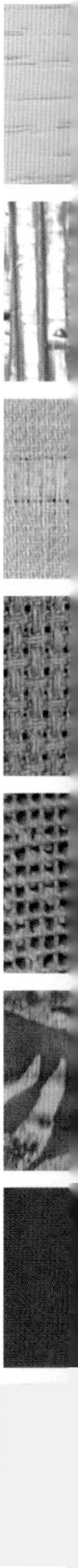

mother-of-pearl
coral
bleached woods
fresh crisp linen
light breeze
cascading water

KELLY HOPPEN for **yoo**

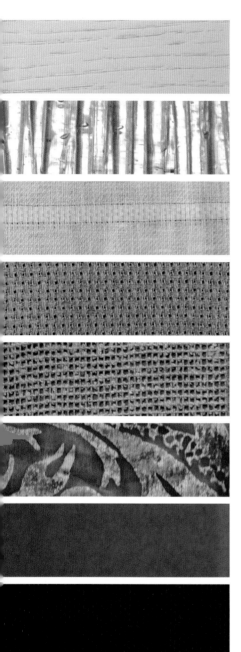

SEA BREEZES

"Interestingly," begins Kelly Hoppen, "thinking about this scheme drew on methods that are already very close to my instinctive way of creating. On a subliminal level I am very sensitive to the natural world, and find its influence frequently apparent in my designs. A staircase may follow the lines of a conch shell, or I may use a shimmering highlight that might be inspired by a ray of light dancing on water."

A sense of place and time, however, also became important when Hoppen began to consider the atmosphere she wanted to invoke for this particular concept. "This palette recalls the simplicity and relaxed cool of a very special holiday home," says Hoppen. "I wanted to catch the essence of a light sea breeze after the heat of the day." The white and taupe palette for fabrics and paint is set against the gnarled texture of driftwood and pearlescent shells. The edge of classic Hoppen design is introduced with chrome, natural stone and sparkling hurricane lights. "It's a really cool, fresh palette," says Hoppen. "When I think about the sea and sun I really want very simple things, a very uncluttered environment that gives me space to unwind. A retreat by the sea should be simple and peaceful. I hate clutter in the heat."

Hoppen's choice of fabrics was directed by this sense of lightness, manifesting in window treatments, such as fluttering linen voiles, and the absence of her other trademark materials, such as heavy velvet drapes. "But it is important to keep varying the texture," says Hoppen. "This adds interest and depth to the scheme. Some weights of fabric are thicker than others, some darker in tone, but all of them are in some way complementary."

Hoppen also created a sense of serenity by using what she describes as "Clean-cut organic-shaped furniture. It's still minimal, but not hard-edged, and as a result has a sort of 'connection with nature' feel." Hoppen's other materials of choice, the horn and shell fastenings that she frequently uses on her cushions, also make a fitting appearance. The natural element is always carefully controlled, however, by taking the form of sharp-edged bands, or by being repetitiously featured on linen cushions. "The irregular edges of the shells, and knots in the wood, give areas of unexpected interest. And in a way the discipline of the forms actually accentuates these qualities."

Selecting and using shades of white

"White is unashamedly high maintenance, which is why it has come to be associated with luxury," says Hoppen. "But it is also quite misunderstood. White is not a static colour. To the trained eye it comes in a huge spectrum of hue and tone. Just taking several samples and comparing them will illustrate the point beautifully. White also mixes very well with both the sand and taupe families, which give range and contrast to the scheme." When choosing a white, look carefully at the underlying base tint and whether it has a pink, blue or yellow cast. If you select a cream white, for example, choose your other decorating elements to correspond to a warm palette

ABOVE The Sea Breezes palette is fresh and light, combining blue-toned whites, stone, taupe and sand colours mixed with chrome, glass, mother-of-pearl and metallics. Texture is achieved with the use of board flooring and open-weave fabrics such as linen.

to give a more unified look. White reflects light more than any other colour, so the finish you choose will affect how it looks – glossier whites often work in crisp, modern spaces, while satin finishes are softer. Hoppen is a great proponent of the use of texture for variation in an all-white scheme. "I use horn buttons, for example, or a very thick weight and an uneven grain of linen, which lends a tactile quality. This idea extends to wools, cashmere and wood, where as lacquers, marbles and linen are cool." This attention to the ambient feelings created by material is what transforms a cold, white room into a place of comfort and intimacy.

Using the correct lighting is essential to warm up a white interior. "I really believe that a very well-thought-through lighting scheme is some of the best money that can be spent on an interiors scheme," enthuses Hoppen. "It has a huge effect on the impact of the other elements, and can bring out the best in crushed velvet or parachute fabrics. It also completely changes the mood of a room and has the added advantage of making you look great. I always say if you can't look good in your own home, where can you?" Hoppen suggests a variety of lighting treatments to give the best, most adaptable results. "The great thing about lighting," she adds, "is that it's almost like jewellery. You can add it or take it away, creating varying moods and effects. I also think that Anglepoise lamps or vintage pieces are a great way to evolve a room; you can swap them in or add as you come across something special."

"You have to appreciate that any room you are tackling will be seen at different times of the day and night. That means it needs to work with harsh midday glare as well as manage the very different light quality of evening electric light. I rarely use overhead lighting as it is stark and jarring. Diffused light from concealed lighting, or a pendant lamp hung low over a table is much more effective at creating a welcoming mood. And lighting can serve no obvious practical purpose by taking some very sculptural forms, but when the main lights are turned off they can be very effective at creating areas of interest and shadows." It's also worth considering the seasons. "A white room can be instantly made more cosy for the cooler months by hanging huge silk curtains as it will be both literally and visually warmer. It's exactly the same principal as rotating your summer wardrobe for your winter one."

A quintessential Hoppen interior employs metal finishes to great effect, and here lies one of the keys to unlocking the mystery of the all-white scheme. "People underestimate just how much influence their choice of materials has on the overall effect. For example, in the Sea Breezes palette I have used chrome to give a highly reflective, clean edge. But brass or bronze would have warmed the scheme, and wrought iron would have given a more muted feel." Hoppen has one more golden rule for the would-be all-white room dweller: "Add some colour. Not a lot, perhaps just an accent piece like a lamp or throw. In a way, because it has something to play off against, it makes the rest of room seem more white."

TOP The freshness of a sea breeze is evoked with natural linen and gentle tones of white. Elegant comfort meets geometric forms in the easy armchair that is positioned on a tactile, textured rug . Various materials and textures in the same colour scheme are juxtaposed to unify the room.

ABOVE Reminiscent of the welcoming beacon of a lighthouse, a row of identical storm lanterns create a flickering focus on a low-level coffee table.

The great thing about lighting is that it's almost like jewellery… you can add it or take it away, creating various moods and effects.

KELLY HOPPEN

What brought you to Yoo?

I've known John Hitchcox for years and he has always been asking me to get involved with the Yoo project. The timing wasn't ever right, because, to be honest, I didn't have any time. Then John wanted me to do a property for his personal use, so that got the ball rolling. From there, we created two further concepts.

Where do you begin with new concepts?

I'm inspired a lot by my travels. I'm naturally very creative and my mind always has ideas popping into it; it's sort of just what I do.

What was different about this project?

Working for an unknown person. When it comes to a specific job I know the client, but in this case I considered how someone might want to use the space, and how I would want to use the space if it was mine.

Where do you begin when presented with a new project?

For a private client, I give them a questionnaire to find out exactly how they will be using the home and what their lifestyle is like. What people think they want and what they need to service their needs are sometimes different. I always make sure that the practical needs of a space are catered for, so if I'm designing a dressing room, for example, I want to know how many Birkin bags they have, their shoe collection and so forth, so I understand what, and how, things should be displayed. I work on these practical issues of a scheme right from the beginning. The architect and I will work together to ensure that it all fits together. That's how really great concept design should work: everything considered from the start.

What advice would you give for beginning an interiors project?

I think it's important to act like a professional. Make a sensible budget, plan out the cost of the physical work, think about the furniture you want and really need; it is when people do things ad hoc that they end up buying mismatched schemes or go well over-budget. Spending a realistic amount of time planning is the key to making the whole project run smoothly and come together. And research is key. When planning a season's wardrobe you would look at magazines and consider what's available, making sure it's a good fit and suits you. Make sure you do the same with design books and journals so that you are not just choosing items without considering the whole look, and that it is in keeping with your personal style.

What do you think people want from today's interior space?

More than just an interior space. It needs to be a home that makes them feel safe and considered. It is no longer just about the surface and how things look. It is much more about connection and how we live.

You are known for your use of neutrals and white. How would you feel about people introducing colour to your palettes?

I have no problem with it. I think what I do well is create an environment that allows others to tastefully represent themselves, against a calm backdrop. I do use colour myself, in the form of perhaps coloured glass or artworks, and I love using flowers in a completed room. I don't like flowers in the garden, but I adore them within the home.

It's all equally important. There isn't a single feature about a space that you don't need to work on from the beginning; the existing architectural features, layout, lighting, the function. Ignore one thing and it can all fall apart.

Tell us one of your favourite insider tips.

Always date your plans so that you, and anyone else working from them, knows which is the latest version. It sounds simple but can save a lot of problems before they happen.

What is your dream future project?

I only take on projects that excite me so in that way they are all dream projects. Having said that, I've never done a project in Brazil. I'd love to make something happen in Brazil.

How would you like people to feel about your schemes?

I would be thrilled if someone said that it had a calming, mood-improving effect on them. I want it to be a space that makes people feel good as well as looking good.

KELLY'S 10 STYLE RULES TO BREAK

1 "Don't overcrowd a room with large furniture." Play with scale. In a large room, large-scale objects fill the space and make it feel more intimate. Even in small rooms a few oversized objects can trick the eye into believing it's bigger than it is.

2 "Listen to your instincts." Plan to the very last detail. Plans might sound boring but they are essential for avoiding costly mistakes. Consider everything from furnishings and lighting to the technology so every element can be brought together in harmony.

3 "Kitchens need bright task lighting." Every room needs a variety of lighting. It's more pleasant to cook an evening meal in a relaxing atmosphere. Use a range of sculptural soft lights and candles to create mood and interesting shadows.

4 "Light colours create space." Dark colours can create a dramatic atmosphere and, when teamed with contrasting fabrics, a sense of indulgence.

5 "Display your favourite objects." Choose the best, store the rest.

6 "Upgrade when you can." Save for what you really want.

7 "Don't fuss with detailing." Use bands and buttons on cushions to freshen up the look of a room. They are an ideal way to unify contrasting colours and textures.

8 "White is the essential neutral." The perfect neutral is taupe. Taupe loves white, natural linens, shades of stone, metal and dark stained wood.

9 "A sofa should be an elegant statement." A sofa also needs to be incredibly comfortable, fit your practical needs and enhance your room. Using L- or U-shaped seating configurations works well and can direct the eye to a focal point such as a fireplace.

10 "Mirrors should be hung over fireplaces." Use them with abandon. Mirrors, glass surfaces and objects that reflect light add depth to a room and allow a play of light

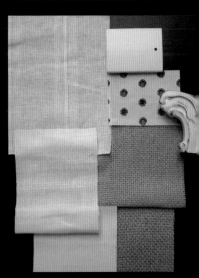

TOP AND ABOVE Kelly's mood boards for the Sea Breezes bathroom palette, top, and bedroom palette, above. Before you begin an interiors project, map out your design ideas by creating a mood board for each room. Collect swatches, clippings and tearsheets of fabrics, paint colours, materials, lighting, accessories, flooring, fixtures and furniture from magazines, manufacturers' brochures or suppliers. Include any details that capture your imagination or develop your concept. Arrange your mood board as a collage on a pinboard or file it in a folder, and keep refining the elements until you achieve a cohesive theme.

BOHO.

paisley
sand
cherry blossom
stone
jim morrison
kerala
lotus
portobello road
teak
vintage
thrift

JADE JAGGER for **yoo**

BOHO

Bohemian is a word that has often been applied to Jade Jagger's sense of personal style. Reflecting the interior of her own home in Ibiza, this scheme conjures up images of long days, hot sun and a relaxed, idiosyncratic approach to enjoying life. The use of hot colours and decorative finishes with clean lines makes the scheme as relevant and applicable to an urban environment as it is to an island retreat.

"Sea, turquoise, lapis, white and orange are all key to creating the right feel," explains Jagger. "It's about taking the sense of relaxation and pleasure while keeping it pared back." One of the decorative elements is achieved with the inclusion of encaustic tiles that are used to create mosaic finishes throughout the house. Instantly recognizable as part of a traditional, Eastern aesthetic, the elaborate geometric patterns throw the surroundings' simple space into unexpected relief.

For the designers, the memories of beach holidays and traveller culture were essential in creating an environment that allows an escape from the city. "This idea of the eclectic traveller was very important to us," says Jagger. "We created an imaginary client to whom the natural world was very important, someone who collects totems that have special meaning to them, like a magpie." The clean white walls create the perfect backdrop in which to show these treasures.

The sensuous simplicity of brushed cotton and burnished silver also creates the sense of quiet luxury. The materials reflect the luxurious sense of calm within this design. Although Jade is almost synonymous with the term "boho", and she has an inherent feel for the style, she feels that the Boho palette does not fully represent her ethos. She explains: "When you are designing, you do find that you draw on your own history or personal preferences, but with each design I feel that they reflect different parts of my, or Tom's personality. That's how you begin to create a clear vision for different themes." Both designers have a love for the hot colours, intricate patternwork and eastern influences that are evoked by the word "bohemian". However, the palette they have created has a much wider and more accessible appeal. They have achieved this by breaking down the dominant threads of vivid colour and pattern, and have created strict restrictions in the way in which it is applied; sparingly and mixed with precision – the minimal bohemian.

Creating relaxed social spaces

When designing a social space, understanding the different ways in which it could be used is key to getting it right. "If you are creating a space for entertaining, it's important to consider how people actually like to relax. Will they be at a table, laying back on cushions, even the time of day; what purposes will it need to serve." Part of the art is forgetting the traditional ideas of entertaining and dining. "Don't be afraid of using big soft pouffes and little tables for holding drinks, in almost a Moroccan approach," continues Tom. "Use a flooring that is inviting, such as soft, thick rugs."

ABOVE A colourful palette that recalls Tunisia and Morocco, Boho combines turquoise, lapis, white and orange. Surface decoration and pattern is achieved by the use of encaustic mosaic tiles and geometrics.

OPPOSITE Olivier Montis swivel chairs by Gijs Papavoine for Architonic are arranged around a black Eero Saarinen Tulip table. The shell-shape of the chairs provides relaxed seating while the neutral backdrop is harmonious and balanced.

"We learnt a lot from creating the communal spaces at the Jade apartments in New York," says Jagger. "For the roof garden we thought a great deal about how to provide intimacy and interest. We achieved this with little terraces." For her interiors, Jagger creates "nooks and crannies and little areas where you can kick back and talk. Really intimate spaces." The team populates the space with furnishings that represent their imaginary "magpie" client; mixing recognizable classics with more rustic finds, such as large Moroccan lamps that cast beguiling shadows.

As any good host can attest, making guests feel good about themselves is a great way to help them relax; this is where lighting can be used to great effect. "Everyone looks better in lamp lighting," laughs Bartlett, "and concealed lighting can be used to create a flattering, indirect light wash. An open fire or fire pit is also a wonderful focus. If you want a sociable space try and ensure your television does not dominate the room."

When it comes to pattern, Jagger and Bartlett are in their element. "We tend not to mix organic pattern and geometrical in the same interior," says Bartlett, "but it is good to mix rhythms, scales and colours if you feel confident. The key is to try and match at least two of these elements." For them, Indian geometry and the souks of Marrakech, with their evocative pigments and designs, provide much inspiration. "We have always loved geometric pattern, partly because of Islamic inspiration and partly through a mutual love of pop art," says Jagger. Geometrics are important to the scheme in unexpected ways. They give the softness of other materials and the prettiness of the glass a harder and more contemporary edge. "What is interesting about using etching on clean-lined contemporary glass or a geometric metal panel is that it creates a very unexpected play of light and shade. It is a delicate, but still bold treatment," says Jagger.

Both Jagger and Bartlett have a deep appreciation for the decorative arts of pattern, and believe that it should be used with "wild abandon." There are, however, some exceptionally effective ways to apply it. "Scale is very important," says Bartlett. "If you have a sample of eighteenth-century toile, for example, blow up a detail of it and use it to cover a contemporary piece of furniture. It creates an unexpected twist. Alternatively, a classical piece of furniture can have huge impact when combined with a very modern covering, such as an op art or fluorescent design."

"The illusions created by playing with scale can be really arresting," explains Jagger. "A small pattern can meld into solid colours when viewed from a distance, and a wide, large-scale patterned rug can link together all the pieces of furniture on it. Pattern used cleverly can really unify a room."

LEFT A mirrored custom table and bench-style seating with Habibi Moroccan lights creates a lounging area that appears refreshing and light in the daytime hours.

OVERLEAF LEFT AND RIGHT Soft furnishings in stripes and animal prints give a harmony of colour, symmetry and line that is underlined by the rectangular architectural elements.

TOP AND ABOVE A white room becomes seductive and moody in the evening as Moroccan lanterns cast deep shadows, while in daytime white walls draw attention to a beautiful wooden door.

ABOVE A view into the dining area from outside this villa in Ibiza. The home is informal but with a strong modernist backdrop, and a fluency between the interior and exterior.

RIGHT Vermilion Gio Ponti 969 chairs are arranged around an MDF Italia table, positioned for a dramatic mountain view.

LEFT A beaded Jesus curtain divides the bathing area from the bedroom, and a floor-to-ceiling mirror creates a feeling of spaciousness.

ABOVE The geometric theme continues throughout this villa, with a mirror and basin standing in front of floor-to-ceiling windows with intersected panes.

LEFT One circular window is reflected in the mirrored walls of the entrance to give the illusion of three windows in a long wall. Similar groupings of colour and repeated pattern are used throughout, with the neutral colour palette acting as support.

ABOVE An example of how a simple limited colourway creates pattern within a rigid linear framework: cubes and geometrics, patterns and solids, are cast against a white, red and black colour scheme in an Ibiza bedroom.

GREEN.

shabby chic
raw woods
crushed linen
vintage tea towels
porcelain
sheepskin
velvet
wrap yourself up and
  be one with nature

KELLY HOPPEN for yoo

GREEN

Although she has designed for luxurious ski lodges, retreats and second homes, a "country-style" interior theme is not a concept immediately associated with Kelly Hoppen. "I had to approach this in a different way. I was trying to create a look for people who want a second home, but that still represented their city sensibility. I have a house in the country, which is very comfortable, and what I want is simplicity and comfort. I think people want to say they spend time in the country, but they are not a bumpkin; that they are still hip."

As expected, the general aesthetic is still pared-back, but a country feel is communicated through subtle tweaks to the original Hoppen style. Creased neutral linens, large plantation shutters, antique Hungarian fabrics, and footstools lend an informal retreat feel; although still more reinterpreted as country house rather than cottage kitsch. "I suppose you could call it shabby chic," says Hoppen. "It has a New England feel. Unlined curtains, whitewashed floors, tongue-and-groove in the kitchen and heavy-duty matting. We've even put damask fabrics in the washing machine to give them an aged feel."

The selection of furniture is also a move away from the classic urban look, which has become known as the standard Hoppen brand. "I've included an interesting mix of vintage and modern furniture," says Hoppen, "which is new for me. Things have progressed with me in terms of what I feel a home should represent. It's important that your home mirrors who you are and that means learning to how to happily assimilate a mix of objects that you may have found, inherited or simply love for a personal reason." These items are still placed within the classic Hoppen contexts of a polished and well-considered backdrop, using the mix of taupes, sand, white and black, but are more forgiving to more weathered personal items. "A home in the city may need to function efficiently and give you the space to clear your mind, but a home in the country can be more meditative and allow you to connect with more simple pleasures. I still don't believe in clutter, but I do think a less formal style can be appropriate."

Symmetry and balance

"I think that the idea of a country look can be misleading" explains Hoppen. "Because it suggests that there may be a representation of something folksy or kitsch. However, if you want to create a relaxed environment, for me, the same rules apply whether renovating a Fifth Avenue New York apartment or a Gloucestershire country retreat," says Hoppen. "Calm and relaxation must be established from the beginning, with a carefully considered approach to symmetry and balance." This East meets West approach to design, for which Hoppen is known, is at the core of her design philosophy. "I do believe in the principals of feng shui and I do believe that creating the right structure and plan is the key to the rest of the scheme. My underlying

ABOVE The Green palette was created with a "shabby chic" concept in mind. It marries a fresh lime colour with neutrals, such as ecru, bone, taupe and coffee. Much use is made of simple, natural materials throughout the decorating scheme, such as tongue-and-groove flooring, wooden shutters, weathered surfaces and unbleached fabrics.

OPPOSITE The simplicity of the palette brings natural country warmth and cosiness to this living area. The sisal floor rug, Kelly's beige velvet-band cushions on the sofa and arrangements of coral in circular vases all add layers of texture. Varying both visual and tactile texture within a tonal palette is essential to avoid the space becoming washed out and bland.

feeling has always been the same. It's all about order, all about harmony. In real terms, that may mean that I make a Japanese-inspired, very linear open unit, a built-in piece of furniture that is beautifully crafted and looks wonderful, even before it has been dressed with objects. We create everything, so that even before a client has moved in the whole space still looks pleasing to the eye. But I think that a house is not your home until you put all your treasures within it."

Hoppen's ideal is to begin with a symmetrical room, but if that is unachievable a clever use of bespoke cabinetwork or shelving may create a more harmonious effect. Finding a point in the room that draws the eye, perhaps an impressive fireplace or artwork, can also draw attention away from any awkward elements. "It is also important to see how objects work on the vertical angle, such as how window treatments and pictures line up, thinking of the room not just on the horizontal plane." Hoppen suggests that a good way to imagine the room in these terms is to create a grid and draw out the space to see how things really interact. "The balance in the room is always more than just spatial," extrapolates Hoppen. "It is present in the way that fabrics, colour and texture are used. There must be a link throughout these aspects to ensure that they all speak as a collective."

Within this concept lies the mix of organic and hard-edged elements, of the vintage and worn sitting comfortably with contemporary, post-modern objects. "I do eclectic design," says Hoppen. "As a result, it doesn't have to always be a modern or classic piece, in the same way that women no longer are dressed by one designer. Lace, cowboy boots and pearls are all perfectly acceptable together stylistically. What has happened in the fashion world has now happened in the home, that sense of mix and match. That is what we have created with this scheme."

It is this sense of the unique and the unexpected that Hoppen thinks ultimately strikes the best balance. "Arresting features, such as making doors floor-to-ceiling in height or using an incredible sculptural light, immediately draw the eye, playing with your sense of proportion and scale," she says. "And they all work brilliantly. But it is that one piece or object that is placed asymmetrical that really throws the rest of a room into focus. That is the great irony; you can't appreciate symmetry without asymmetry. That's also why it works so well within a natural, country environment. It gives a great sense of contrast to the landscape and is naturally pleasing to be in. Surely that's the ultimate purpose of any country retreat?"

TOP Classic louvered shutters are offset with oversized, floor-standing vases that play with the sense of proportion and scale.

ABOVE Creating a warm comforting alcove for relaxation is essential to the atmosphere of a country dwelling. A velvet cushion with circular button on a Thonet bentwood-and-cane chaise longue offers a place for rest while an adjustable floor lamp and large gold resin letters give a more modern contrast.

The balance in a room is always more than just spatial. It is present in the way that fabrics, colour and texture are used. There must be a link… to ensure that they all speak as a collective.

LEFT Small double sinks create symmetry and balance against a tiled background. Visual interest is achieved through the arrangement of coral pieces and natural sponge.

BELOW The blue and white, rough-hewn linen adds an earthy interest to a quietly luxurious bedroom. Four white ceramic planter pots are arranged on a small storage trunk serving as a bedside table.

OVERLEAF Make the most of an out-of-town setting by developing outdoor seating and dining arrangements to enjoy at various times of the day. Maximize natural light inside the home, and create a glimpse of the outdoors from within, by enlarging window and door openings to floor-to-ceiling height.

THE DIRECTORY

SHOPS

UNITED KINGDOM:

Aram
110 Drury Lane
London WC2B 5SG
Tel: (+44) 020 7557 7557
www.aram.co.uk

The Conran Shop
55 Marylebone High Street
London W1U 5HS
Tel: (+44) 020 7723 2223
www.conranshop.co.uk

Decoratum
13-25 Church Street
London NW8 8DT
Tel: (+44) 020 7724 6969
www.decoratum.com

Habitat
196-199 Tottenham Court Road
London W1T 7PJ
Tel: (+44) 08444 99 1122
www.habitat.net

Fritz Hansen
20-22 Rosebery Avenue
London EC1R 4SX
Tel: (+44) 020 7837 2030
www.fritzhansen.com

Heals
The Heals Building
196 Tottenham Court Road
London W1T 7LQ
Tel: (+44) 020 7636 1666
www.heals.co.uk

Kelly Hoppen
The Yard, 102a Chepstow
Road, London W2 5QW
Tel: (+44) 020 7351 1910
www.kellyhoppenretail.com

Ligne Roset
37-39 Commercial Road
London E1 1LF
Tel: (+44) 020 7426 9670
www.ligne-roset-city.co.uk

Living Space
53-55 Fulham High Street
London SW6 3JJ
Tel: (+44) 020 7731 1180
www.livingspaceuk.com

Purves and Purves
6 Cosmur Close
London W12 9SF
Tel: (+44) 020 8838 0200
www.purves.co.uk

Skandium
86 Marylebone High Street
London W1U 4QS
Tel: (+44) 020 7935 2077
www.skandium.com

Twentytwentyone
274 Upper Street
London N1 2UA
Tel: (+44) 020 7288 1996
www.twentytwentyone.com

UNITED STATES:

Domus Design Collection
181 Madison Avenue
New York, NY 10016
Tel: (+1) 212 966 0800
www.ddcnyc.com

Design Within Reach
341 Columbus Avenue
New York, NY 10024
Tel: (+1) 212 799 5900
www.dwr.com

EBHome
200 East Main Street, Mt. Kisco
New York, NY 10549
Tel: (+1) 914 242 7278
www.ebhome.com

Fresh Kills
50 North 6th Street
New York, NY 11211
Tel: (+1) 718 388 8081
www.freshkillsforthepeople.com

The Magazine
1823 Eastshore Highway
Berkeley, CA 94710
Tel: (+1) 510 549 2282
www.themagazine.info

MoMA Design Store
81 Spring Street
New York, NY
Tel: (+1) 646 613 1367
www.momastore.org

Moss
150 Greene Street
New York, NY 10012
Tel: (+1) 212 204 7100
www.mossonline.com

Totem Design
71 Franklin Street
New York, NY 10013
Tel: (+1) 212 925 5506
www.totemdesign.com

AUSTRALIA:

Beclau
Unit 15
198 Young Street
Waterloo, NSW 2017
Tel: (+61) 2 9698 6422
www.beclau.com

De De Ce
263 Liverpool Street
Darlinghurst
Sydney, NSW 2017
Tel: (+61) 2 9360 2722
www.dedece.com

Living Edge
74 Commonwealth Street
Surry Hills
Sydney, NSW 2010
Tel: (+61) 2 9212 3542
www.livingedge.com.au

Scandinavium
200 Campbell Street,
Darlinghurst
Sydney, NSW 2010
Tel: (+61) 2 9332 4660
www.scandinavium.com.au

Space Furniture
629 Church Street
Richmond, Melbourne
VIC 3121
Tel: (+61) 3 9426 3000
www.spacefurniture.com.au

SUPPLIERS

Accademia
Via Independenza, 4
33044 Manzano, Italy
Tel: (+39) 0432 754439
www.accademiaitaly.com

Adelta
Friedrich-Ebert-Strasse 96
46535 Dinslaken, Germany
Tel: (+49) 02064 40797
www.adelta.de

Alessi
Via Privata Alessi, 6
28882 Crusinallo (Vb), Italy
Tel: (+39) 0323 868611
www.alessi.com

Alias
Via del Videtti, 2
24064 Grumello Del Monte, Italy
Tel: (+39) 035 44 22 511
www.aliasdesign.it

Allermuir
Branch Road, Lower Darwen
Lancashire BB3 0PR
Tel: (+44) 01254 682421
www.allermuir.com

Andreu World
46370 Valencia, Spain
Tel: (+34) 961 805 700
www.andreuworld.com

Arflex
Via Beretta, 12
20034 Giussano (MI), Italy
Tel: (+39) 0362 853043
www.arflex.it

Arper
Via Calalta, 31057
Selio, Treviso, Italy
Tel: (+39) 0422 362638
www.arper.com

Artek
Hiekkakiventie 3
710 Helsinki, Finland
Tel: (+358) 0 613 250
www.artek.fi

Artifort
Van Leeuwenhoekweg 20
5482 TK Schijndel
Netherlands
Tel: (+31) 73 658 00 20
www.artifort.com

Asiatides
11 rue de Cambrai
75019 Paris, France
Tel: (+33) 01 40 05 11 12
www.asiatides.com

Ashworth
11 bd de la Tour Maubourg
75007 Paris, France
Tel: (+33) 145 55 45 65

Astuguevieille
10 rue Portalis
75008 Paris, France
Tel: (+33) 144 699 140

Baas & den Herder BV
Rosmalensedikj 3
5236 BD
's-Hertogenbosch (Gewande)
Netherlands
Tel: (+31) 6 3449 2892
www.maartenbaas.com

Baleri
Via S.Bernadino
24040 Lallio, Bergamo, Italy
Tel: (+39) 035 698 011
www.baleri-italia.com

B&B Italia
22060 Novedrate (CO) Italia
Strada Provinciale 32, Italy
Tel: (+39) 031 795 111
www.bebitalia.it

Bel Air
Amsteldijk Zuid 78 c
1184 VE Amstelveen
Netherlands
Tel: (+31) 20 49 65 038
www.jolina.com

Bonacina Vittorio
Via Madonnina, 12
22040 Lurago D'erba
(Como) Italy
Tel: (+39) 031 699 800
www.bonacinavittorio.it

Boog Thomas
52 rue de Bourgogne
75007 Paris, France
Tel: (+33) 1 47 70 98 10
www.thomasboog.com

Deborah Bowness Wallpaper
Tel: (+44) 07817 807504
www.deborahbowness.com

Cappellini
Via Marconi
35 22060 Arosio, Italy
Tel: (+39) 031 759 111
www.capellini.com

Carrara Marble
45-47 Standard Road
London NW10 6HF
Tel: (+44) 020 8838 4604
www.carraramarble.co.uk

Cassina
Via Busnelli, 1
I-20036 Meda
Milan, Italy
Tel: (+39) 0362 372 1
www.cassina.it

Ceccotti
Viale Sicilia 4/A
56021 Cascina (PI), Italy
Tel: (+39) 050 701 955
www.ceccotti.it

Colourline
Westerstraat 187 (2nd Floor)
1015 MA, Amsterdam
The Netherlands
Tel: (+31) 035 628 28 62
www.colourline.nl

Csao Gallery
1 rue Elzevir
75003 Paris, France
Tel: (+33) 1 44 54 90 50
www.csao.fr

De Padova
Corso Venezia, 14
20121 Milan, Italy
Tel: (+39) 02 777 201
www.depadova.com

Driade
Via Padana Inferiore, 12
29012 Fossadello di Caorso
(PC), Italy
Tel: (+39) 0523 818 660
www.driade.com

Droog Design
Staalstraat 7a/b
1011 JJ Amsterdam
Netherlands
Tel: (+31) 020 523 5050
www.droog.com

Edra
Via Ciovassino, 3
(Brera zone) Milan, Italy
Tel: (+39) 0286 995 122
www.edra.com

Emeco
Piazza Borromeo, 12
20123 Milan, Italy
Tel: (+39) 02 8068871
www.emeco.net

Ercuis
8 bis rue Boissy d'Anglas
75008 Paris, France
Tel: (+33) 01 40 17 03 20
www.ercuis.com

Established and Sons
29/31 Cowper Street
London EC2A 4AT
Tel: (+44) 020 7608 0990
www.establishedandsons.com

Fasem
Via Francesca Nord, 44/46/48
56010 Vicopisano, Pisa, Italy
Tel: (+39) 050 799 576
www.fasem.it

Flexform
Via Einaudi, 23/25
20036 Meda, Italy
Tel: (+39) 0362 3991
www.flexform.it

Flos Lighting
www.flos.com

Fornasetti
Corso Matteotti, 1/A-20121
Milan, Italy
Tel: (+39) 02 8965 8040
www.fornasetti.com

Fratelli Barbini
Fondamenta Serenella
Calle Bertolini, 36
30141 Murano-Venice
Italy
Tel: (+39) 041 739 777
www.fratellibarbini.com

Fritz Hansen
135 bd Raspail
75006 Paris, France
Tel: (+33) 145 4855 74
www.fritzhansen.com

Gärsnäs
Rodbodtorget 2 SE-111 52
Stockholm, Sweden
Tel: (+46) 8 442 91 50
www.garsnas.se

Gervasoni
Zona Industrielle Udinese
33050 Pavia di Udine, Italy
Tel: (+39) 0432 656611
www.gervasoni1882.com

Natanel Gluska
Sägestrasse 28a
5600 Lenzburg, Switzerland
Tel: (+41) 79 691 89 40
www.natanelgluska.com

Graham & Brown
PO Box 39
India Mill
Harwood Street
Blackburn
Lancashire BB1 3DB
Tel: (+44) 0800 328 8452
www.grahambrown.com

Carl Hansen & Son
Holmevaenget 8
5560 Aarup, Denmark
Tel: (+45) 6612 1404
www.carlhansen.com

Interlubke
Hauptstraße 74
33373 Rheda-Wiedenbruck
Germany
Tel: (+49) 052 42 12 1
www.interlubke.de

Isokon Plus
Turnham Green
Terrace Mews, Chiswick
London W4 1QU
Tel: (+44) 020 8994 7032
www.isokonplus.com

Kartell
Via Porta Carlo, 1
20121 Milan, Italy
Tel: (+39) 02 2901 4935
www.kartell.it

Knoll
268 bd Saint Germain
75005 Paris, France
Tel: (+33) 01 44 18 19 63
www.knollint.com

Living Divani
Strada del Cavolto
22040 Anzano del Parco Co
Italy
Tel: (+39) 031 630954
www.livingdivani.it

Lorna Lee John Muller
15 West 53rd Street
New York, NY 10019
Tel: (+1) 212 397 3803
www.lornaleejohnmullerdesigns.
com

Magis
Via Magnadola, 15
31045 Motta di Livenza (TV)
Italy
Tel: (+39) 0422 862600
www.magisdesign.com

Herman Miller
Methuen Park
Chippenham SN14 0GF
Tel: +44 0845 226 7201
www.hermanmiller.com

Minotti
Via Indipendenza, 152
P O Box 61
20036 Meda Mi, Italy
Tel: (+39) 0362 343 499
www.minotti.com

Modernica
7366 Beverly Boulevard
Los Angeles, CA 90036, USA
Tel: (+1) 213 933 0383
www.users.aol.com/modernica

Moooi
Minervum 7003
4817 ZL, PO Box 5703
4801 EC
Breda, Netherlands
Tel: (+31) 76 578 4444
www.moooi.nl

Molteni
Via Rossini, 50
20034 Giussano
Milan, Italy
Tel: (+39) 0362 359 1
www.molteni.it

Moroso
Via Nazionale, 60-33010
Udine, Italy
Tel: (+39) 0432 577 111
www.moroso.it

Nord Sud
Les Bois du Cerf
91450, Etoilles, France
Tel: (+33) 01 69 89 09 14

Offecct
Box 100, SE-543 21
Tibrom, Sweden
Tel: (+46) 504 415 00
www.offecct.se

Promemoria
Via Roma, 47
23900 Lecco, Italy
Tel: (+39) 0341 366 197
www.promemoria.com

Quodes
Tel: (+31) 0 23 533 7 533
www.quodes.com

Rêves du Désert
Sahraï Srl
Via G. Verdi, 5
20121 Milano, Italy
Tel: (+39) 0039 02 43 51 05 30
www.revesdudesert.com

Sia
www.sia-collection.com

Sawaya & Moroni
Via Manzoni, 11
20121 Milan, Italy
Tel: (+39) 02863951
www.sawayamoroni.com

Squeeze
19 Kim Chuan Terrace
537041, Singapore
Tel: (+65) 9765 8455
www.squeezedesign.com

Studio Jon Male
Arch 3
Corporation Street
Manchester M4 4DG
Tel: (+44) 0161 832 1442
www.studiojonmale.com

Tecta
D-37697 Lauenförde
Sohnreystr 10, Germany
Tel: (+49) 05273 37 89 0
www.tecta.de

Pascal Tarabay
www.pascaltarabay.com
Available from:
www.leighharmer.co.uk

Thonet
Michael-Thonet-Strasse 1
35066 Frankenberg, Germany
Tel: (+49) 064 51 508 119
www.thonet.com

Tolix
Bd Bernard Giberstein
71400 Autun, France
Tel: (+33) 03 85 86 96 70
www.tolix.fr

Triangolo
Via della Resistenza sc
61030 Calcinelli di Saltara
(PU), Italy
Tel: (+39) 0721 878511
www.triangolo.com

Toulemonde Bochart
10 rue du Mail
75002 Paris, France
Tel: (+33) 1 40 26 68 83

Unifor
Via Isonzo, 1
22078 Turate, Como, Italy
Tel: (+39) 02967191
www.unifor.it

Up + Up
Tel: (+39) 585 8311 32
www.upgroup.it

Vitra
40 rue Violet
75015 Paris, France
Tel: (+33) 01 45 75 59 11
www.vitra.com

Vitsoe
72 Wigmore Street
London W1U 2SG
Tel: (+44) 020 7935 4968
www.vitsoe.com

XO
77170 Servon, France
Tel: (+33) 01 60 62 60 60
www.xo-design.com

Ycami
Via Provinciale, 31
22060, Novedrate, Como, Italy
Tel: (+39) 031 79 02 93
www.ycami.com

Zanotta
Via Vittorio Veneto, 57
20054 Nova Milanese, Italy
Tel: (+39) 0362 4981
www.zanotta.it

WEBSITES

Mydeco
For room planning, interior
design advice and products.
http://mydeco.com

Designers
www.kellyhoppenretail.com
www.marcelwanders.com
www.starck.com
www.yoo.com

PROJECT DIRECTORY

74 GRANGE ROAD,
Singapore
74 Grange Road, Singapore
Partner: Heeton Holdings

THE ADAM, Split
Bacvice Beach
Split, Croatia
Partner: Spectator Grupa

CAPE YAMU, Phuket
Phuket, Thailand
Partner: Campbell Kane

**DOWNTOWN BY
STARCK,** New York
15 Broad Street
New York, NY, USA
Partner: Boymelgreen
Developers

DWELL 95, New York
95 Wall Street
New York, NY, USA
Partner: The Moinian Group

EURASIA TOWER, Moscow
12 MIBC, Moscow-City, Russia
Partner: Eurasia Group

G-TOWER DUBAI, Dubai
Dubailand, Dubai, UAE
Partner: Galadari Investment
Office Ltd.

GRAMERCY, New York
340 East 23rd Street
New York, NY, USA
Partner: Victor Homes

THE HOUSE, Dallas
The Victory Park Discovery
Center, 2512 Cedar Springs,
Dallas, TX, USA
Partner: Hillwood Capital

ICON BRICKELL, Miami
465 Brickell Avenue
Miami, FL, USA
Partner: The Related Group

ICON SOUTH BEACH,
South Beach
450 Alton Road
South Beach, FL, USA
Partner: The Related Group

ICON VALLARTA, Mexico
Blvd. Francisco Medina
Ascencio y Av. de las Garzas,
Puerto Vallarta, Jalisco C.P.
48300, Mexico
Partner: The Related Group

THE JADE, New York
16W 19th Street
New York, NY, USA
Partner: The Copper Group Inc.

JADE JAGGER FOR YOO,
Marrakech
Road to Amizmiz, Marrakech,
Morocco
Partner: Ajensa

JIA, Hong Kong
1-5 Irving Street, Causeway
Bay, Hong Kong, China
Partner: JIA Boutique Hotels

THE LAKES, Gloucester
Coln Park, Claydon Pike, Near
Lechlade, Gloucester, UK
Partner: The Raven Group

LEONTIEVSKY MYS,
St Petersburg
Zhdanovskaja str., 45,
St Petersburg, Russia
Partner: Dronokov

MANOR MILLS, Leeds
Holbeck Village, Leeds, UK
Partner: Yoo Capital

MANYOO, Manchester
Harbour City, Salford Keys,
Manchester, UK
Partner: Yoo Capital

THE MERTASARI, Bali
Jalan Mertasari, Sanur,
Denpasar, Bali 80228, Indonesia
Partner: Oriental & Occidental
Developments

META, Sydney
21 Brisbane Street, Surry Hills
NSW 2010, Australia
Partner: Carrington Group

NW8, London
17 Hall Road, London, UK
Partner: Yoo Capital

OBZOR, Bulgaria
21 Marie Louisa Boulevard,
9000 Varna, Bulgaria
Partner: Unique Developments

PARRIS LANDING, Boston
42 Eighth Street, Charlestown
Boston, MA, USA
Partner: Carlyle

SEVENTY5 PORTLAND,
Toronto
75 Portland Street
Toronto, ONT, Canada
Partner: Freed Developments

TRIBECA, Melbourne
Powlett Street
East Melbourne, Australia
Partner: R Corporation

**VILAMOURA GOLF
RESORT**, Portugal
Morgado da Lameira, 8365-023
Alcantarilha, Algarve, Portugal
Partner: Oceanico Group

YooD4, Boston
7 Warren Avenue
Boston, MA, USA
Partner: Urbanica, Developer

Yoo HAMBURG, Hamburg
Hafencity, Am Dalmannkai,
20457 Hamburg, Germany
Partner: Yoo Deutschland

Yoo ISTANBUL, Istanbul
Zincirlikuyu, Istanbul, Turkey
Partner: Say Developments

Yoo MUNICH, Munich
Thalkirchner Strasse 54, 80337
Munich, Germany
Partner: Yoo Deutschland

Yoo PANAMA, Panama City
Balboa Avenue
Panama City, Panama
Partners: Habitats Realty,
Consorcio General,
Centurion Realty

Yoo PHUKET, Phuket
Kathu District
Phuket, Thailand
Partner: Absolute
Developments

Yoo PUNE, India
Koregaon Park Annex,
Hadapsar, Pune
Maharashtra, India
Partner: Panchshil Realty

Yoo PUNTA DEL ESTE,
Uruguay
Av. Roosevelt, Parada 8
Punta del Este, Uruguay
Partner: K Group

Yoo TEL AVIV, Tel Aviv
Northern District
Tel Aviv, Israel
Partner: Habas Group

ACKNOWLEDGEMENTS

Yoo would like to thank the following people:
Philippe Starck, Jade Jagger, Marcel Wanders, Kelly Hoppen, Tom Bartlett, Lisa Dyer, Clare Baggaley, Jasmine Starck, Karin Krautgartner, Eva James, Goska Sobkowiak, Leila Naghashi, Camille Pichon, Victoria Smith, Sarah Hocken, Sally Saunders, Alison Antrobus, and especially to all of our development partners and everyone at Yoo.

The publishers would like to thank the Yoo team, especially John Hitchcox, Rachelle Munsie, Mark Davison and Julieann Humphreys, for making this book possible. Many thanks also go to the team of contributing writers who have written the palette sections and interview pages. They are:

MARCUS FAIRS
for Marcel Wanders

Formerly founding editor of the architecture and design magazine, icon, Marcus is currently editor of online design magazine *Dezeen* (www.dezeen.com). A journalist, lecturer and curator, he wrote about architecture and design for a number of British publications including *Blueprint, The Guardian, The Independent on Sunday* and *Condé Nast Traveller*.

LISA HELMANIS
for Jade Jagger and Kelly Hoppen

Lisa is an author, photographer, stylist and television presenter. Formerly editorial director of Mydeco.com, she has also been editor of *Inside Out* magazine UK, and lifestyle editor of *Living etc., She* magazine and *Condé Nast Brides*.

VICTORIA O'BRIEN
for Yoo Design Studio

An interiors journalist who worked for over ten years as a design correspondent for both *The Times* and *The Sunday Times*, Victoria has contributed to a variety of publications, including *The Daily Telegraph, Homes & Gardens* and *Living etc.*

FAY SWEET
for Philippe Starck

An authority on the history of modern design and architecture, Fay works as a journalist and broadcaster, and is the author of more than 30 design- and architecture-related books, including *Vintage Furniture* and *Philippe Starck: Subverchic Design*.

PICTURE CREDITS

Carlton Books and Yoo would like to thank the following sources for their kind permission to reproduce the pictures in this book.

Key: t=Top, b=Bottom, c=Centre, l=Left and r=Right

9t Getty Images/Wayne R Bilenduke; 9b Magnum/Ferdinando Scianna; 10 Corbis/Ted Streshinsky; 14 Lonely Planet Images/ Greg Elms; 17t Lonely Planet Images/Mitch Reardon; 17c Corbis/Reuters/Mariana Bazo; 22 Getty Images/Matt Henry Gunther; 46 Photolibrary/Ada Summer; 66 Corbis/Arcaid; 80 istockphoto.com/William Britten; 85t The Bridgeman Art Library/Musée d'Orsay, Paris, France; 92 istockphoto.com; 96 Getty Images/Glen Allison; 104 Getty Images; 112 Corbis/ Wes Thompson; 128 Getty Images/Hans Christian Heap; 140 Photolibrary/Don Johnston; 148 Photolibrary/Steve Mason; 154 Photolibrary/Marcel Jolibois; 174 Getty Images/Kristina Kontoniemi

All the following images are provided by Yoo, as indicated.

Hardback cover: front, Claudia Uribe; back, Courtesy of Marcel Wanders Studio.
Dust jacket and paperback cover: front cover, Claudia Uribe; back cover, Claudia Uribe; front flap: Paul Roy; back flap: photograph of John Hitchcox, Jorkaim Blockstrom; photograph of Philippe Starck, Jean-Baptiste Mondinio; photograph of Kelly Hoppen, Courtesy of Kelly Hoppen; photograph of Jade Jagger, Robert Astley-Sparke; photograph of Marcel Wanders, Joakim Blockstrom.
Endpapers: photography Studio 4 @ www.photostudio4.co.uk

1 Claudia Uribe; 2 Mel Yates; 4 ©Paúl Rivera/archphoto.com; 5–6 Courtesy of Marcel Wanders Studio; 11 Jorkaim Blockstrom; 12t seventh art ©2003; 12b ©Paúl Rivera/archphoto.com; 13 seventh art ©2003; 15 Grischa Rüeschendorf/rupho;16t and 16b Jaimie Travezan; 17b Courtesy of Jade Jagger; 18t Robert Astley Sparke; 18b Courtesy of Marcel Wanders Studio; 19 Joth Shakerley; 20–1 Paul Roy; 25 Claudia Uribe; 26t ©Paúl Rivera/archphoto.com; 26b www.methanoia.com; 27t, c and b Claudia Uribe; 28 Claudia Uribe; 29 Claudia Uribe; 30–1 Michael Smallcombe; 32 Michael Smallcombe; 33 Michael Smallcombe; 34 Julieanne Humphryes; 35 ©Paúl Rivera/archphoto.com; 36t Jean-Baptiste Mondino; 37t TR Paul Harmer; 38 Courtesy of Marcel Wanders Studio; 41–5

Courtesy of Marcel Wanders Studio; 49 Michael Smallcombe; 50–1 Claudia Uribe; 52 H.G. Esch, Hennef-Stadt Blankenberg; 53 Michael Smallcombe; 54 Claudia Uribe; 56 Michael Smallcombe; 57t Paul Harmer; 57b Michael Smallcombe; 58 Courtesy of Marcel Wanders Studio; 61t Courtesy of Marcel Wanders Studio; 61b Federico Cedrone; 62t Federico Cedrone; 62b Courtesy of Marcel Wanders Studio; 63–5 Courtesy of Marcel Wanders Studio; 69–70 Richard Leeney; 71 Ed Reeve; 72–3 Richard Leeney; 74 Flos, Piero Fasanotto; 77–9 Courtesy of Marcel Wanders Studio; 83 - Claudia Uribe; 84 Paul Roy; 86 ©Paúl Rivera/archphoto.com; 87 ©Paul Rivera/archphoto.com; 88t Zoltan Prepszent; 88–9 Michael Smallcombe; 90 Michael Smallcombe; 91 Paul Harmer; 95t Paul Roy; 95b Richard Leeney; 99 ©Paúl Rivera/archphoto.com; 100–103 ©Paúl Rivera/ archphoto.com; 107t Jorkaim Blockstrom; 107b Richard Leeney; 108 Paul Harmer; 109t Paul Harmer; 109b Jorkaim Blockstrom; 115–119 Courtesy of Kelly Hoppen Interiors; 120 ©Paúl Rivera/ archphoto.com; 123–5 ©Paúl Rivera/archphoto.com; 126t Robert Astley Sparke; 126b Waldo Works Studio; 127b Ed Reeve; 131–2 H.G.Esch, Hennef-Stadt Blankenberg; 133t David Archer; 133b Michael Smallcombe; 134–5 Michael Smallcombe; 136 Claudia Uribe; 137 ©Paúl Rivera/archphoto.com; 138–9 H.G.Esch, Hennef-Stadt Blankenberg; 143–5 Courtesy of Marcel Wanders Studio; 146 Sebastiaan Westerweel; 147 Inga Powilleit, styling by Tatjana Quax; 151–3 Richard Leeney; 157–9 Courtesy of Kelly Hoppen Interiors; 160 Courtesy of Jade Jagger; 163–73 Ed Reeve; 177–81 – Mel Yates; 182 – Ed Reeve; 184 from top: Courtesy of Marcel Wanders Studio, Ed Reeve, Courtesy of Marcel Wanders Studio, ©Paúl Rivera/archphoto.com; 185 from top: Courtesy of Marcel Wanders Studio, Michael Smallcombe, Courtesy of Kelly Hoppen Interiors, Claudia Uribe;186 from top: ©Paúl Rivera/archphoto.com, Claudia Uribe, Claudia Uribe, Michael Smallcombe;187t, c: Pixel Arquitectura; 187b ©Paúl Rivera/ archphoto.com; 192 Claudia Uribe.

Every effort has been made to acknowledge correctly and contact the source and/or copyright holder of each picture and Carlton Books Limited apologizes for any unintentional errors or omissions which will be corrected in future editions of this book.

INDEX